MAKING SENSE OF MYTH AND MYTHOPOEIA

A GUIDE TO ANALYSIS AND INTERPRETATION

EDITED BY
SUJATHA ARAVINDAKSHAN MENON
A. YUVARAJ

BLUEROSE PUBLISHERS
India | U.K.

Copyright © Sujatha Aravindakshan Menon, A Yuvaraj 2024

All rights reserved by author. No part of this publication may be reproduced, stored in a retrieval system or transmitted in any form or by any means, electronic, mechanical, photocopying, recording or otherwise, without the prior permission of the author. Although every precaution has been taken to verify the accuracy of the information contained herein, the publisher assumes no responsibility for any errors or omissions. No liability is assumed for damages that may result from the use of information contained within.

BlueRose Publishers takes no responsibility for any damages, losses, or liabilities that may arise from the use or misuse of the information, products, or services provided in this publication.

For permissions requests or inquiries regarding this publication, please contact:

BLUEROSE PUBLISHERS
www.BlueRoseONE.com
info@bluerosepublishers.com
+91 8882 898 898
+4407342408967

ISBN: 978-93-5989-974-9

Cover design: Tahira
Typesetting: Tanya Raj Upadhyay

First Edition: February 2024

Dedicated to all dear and near who have supported and encouraged us (including our dear departed who watch over us from above)

Disclaimer

This book is written purely for academic purposes and does not intend to question anyone's beliefs or sentiments.

Foreword

The word myth evokes a euphoric feeling among myth lovers and a smirk among those who find them nothing but glorified jabberwocky. The literary world and the visual media, however, hold a different opinion. The majority of fiction published these days is mythopoeic, which accounts for the fact that it is the genre that readers find riveting although the stories contained therein may be lies breathed through silver. Reading stories and novels centred on mythological characters is fascinating no doubt, but there is a dearth of books that deal with ways of decoding and deciphering mythical renderings or revisionist mythopoesis as we may call it.

This book intends to be a solution to critics and researchers who are interested in myth and mythopoeia. It was originally meant to be an anthology containing at least twenty research articles. But then I decided that merely reading articles would not help researchers in writing a research article. So, the book must be structured differently. The consequence is that the book has authors airing their views on myth and mythopoeia, researchers voicing their opinions on mythopoeic texts, editors explaining how texts should be interpreted and how an essay can be converted into a research article, and book reporters/ reviewers reviewing a book or presenting a report on it.

It will be a gross injustice if I don't acknowledge the efforts of everyone whose name appears in this book. I thank them wholeheartedly for agreeing to be a part of this venture. Anand Neelakantan was working at a neck-break pace on other ventures amidst which he squeezed in time to pen his views and email them. Anuja Chandramouli was delighted with the venture and was the first to send her views. Swarnalatha Rangarajan is way too sweet to refuse a friend. Her story arrived on my birthday in my inbox and that was a gift to cherish. Ampat Koshy is a mentor and friend who is ever-ready when it comes to creativity.

Yuvaraj, my co-editor, was the real stress buster in the whole venture. He offered suggestions, argued on formats, and comforted me whenever I thought the work was getting on my nerves. Professor Vinod Balakrishnan who agreed to write the introduction is humility personified. He constantly boosted my morale, saying everything would be okay.

My mother Radha Lakshmi and my daughter Varshaa deserve special thanks for their patience in enduring my closed-room penance. Their understanding was the best inspiration I could ever wish for. Thanks to my friends, colleagues, and other well-wishers for spurring me to finish what I had taken up.

Thanks to God and all who supported me, my dream has transformed into a reality like Pygmalion's Galatea.

Sujatha Aravindakshan Menon

Table of Contents

Foreword vii
Introduction 1

The Artefact and the Artisan 8

Myth, Culture, and Women in India 9
Anand Neelakantan

Mythology and Me 13
Anuja Chandramouli

Sita's Hypothesis 17
Swarnalatha Rangarajan

Hector, O, Hector! 40
A.V. Koshy

The Editor's Workshop 42

Voicing the Voiceless: Views on *The Penelopiad* 44
Lakshmi Krishna Kumar

Analysing and Interpreting *Sita's Hypothesis* 59
Sujatha Aravindakshan Menon

Deciphering 'Hector, O, Hector!' 65
A. Yuvaraj

The Critic/ Researcher 69

Making Sense of Myth and Mythopoeia 70
Sujatha Aravindakshan Menon

Ahalya's 'Awakening' in the Twenty- First Century 90
Anjitha Anil and Sushant Kishore

Exploring Mythmaking in Chokshi's *Star-Touched Stories* 102
A.R. Chitra

Book Reports/Reviews 116

Robert A. Segal's *Myth: A Very Short Introduction* A Book Report..117
Fr. Joby Joseph

Anand Neelakantan's *Nala Damayanti* 123
R. Durga and S. Barathi

Natalie Haynes' *Stone Blind* 125
A. Yuvaraj

Afterword..*128*

Introduction

Vinod Balakrishnan

What the biologist has not yet declared but will not dismiss, is the truth that our capacity for mythmaking is sewn into the DNA. Our moments of dread, confusion, moral dilemmas, and incredulity have not only triggered adrenaline rushes, but have also triggered the latent elements of our first stories. We work our way through the dark corridors of life by making stories. Like the stories of Scheherazade, they are lifelines out of our imminent death. We work out of existential darkness holding the clue of our stories, like Ariadne's thread that helped Theseus navigate his fate out of the Minotaur's labyrinth. We are seekers who seek meaning. In pursuit of meaning, we made, and continue to make stories. Like dung beetles that dab bites of clay till they roll it into smooth balls, we dab our everyday bafflements with the clay of symbols till they smoothly roll out as myths.

Myth or mythmaking has had a difficult relationship with science. That is because the first mythmakers did not possess the method or the technology to explain the phenomena of the circumambient universe. By our reckoning, it was a different universe built out of pure imagination. Further, our myth-making forefathers employed imagination to make sense of their universe. Myth or mythmaking has had an equally difficult relationship with history. Every day was a measure of the community's capacity to survive existential odds. It never had the luxury of a Hegel to reflect on history as an idea or an epistemic spreadsheet. A contingent reality limited the community's engagement with history to decoding the seasons and recurrent natural phenomena. Mythmakers developed capacities like being able to spot Venus in broad daylight and made more stories out of phenomenal patterns. The stories of a tribe, strangely, resembled those of the other tribes even when the tribes themselves were scattered. No two mythmakers, belonging to different tribes, ever told their stories to each other. Yet they spun identical stories out of their struggle to survive calamities.

We have travelled a great distance, historically, making stories out of every day, mythologically, and decoding their significance for mankind. The task of decoding has been the lifetime mission for some remarkable men who walked away from the distracting bustle of coffee house banter, conversations in well-appointed salons as well as the dizzying ambience of literary and philosophical clubs. One distinctly remembers the journeys of Claude Lévi-Strauss, Malinowski and Lévy-Bruhl. One also remembers Mircea Eliade's journeys in pursuit of religions across cultures and climes. Philosophers like C.G Jung, semiologists like Roman Jakobson and Roland Barthes, and mythographers like Heinrich Zimmer, Joseph Campbell, G.S Frazer and Jesse Weston have viewed myths from different perspectives thereby enriching our understanding.

The chief value of myths for the race of human beings is the furtherance of our understanding of ourselves. To Erich Fromm, the pursuit of myths facilitated an extensive study of humans thus viewing it as "a message from ourselves to ourselves." Just as humans have an appearance on the surface but a reality buried in layers like a palimpsest, myths have a surface manifestation that encodes their potential significance several feet under the sign. In the post humanist era, humans have lost all innocence, and stagger under the weight of existence, only too aware of the soul they have forfeited to contingency in the manner of a Faust. So, they must stumble through the panorama of anarchy to pick up the broken pieces of an existence that was once in order. The modern writer as the mirror and the lamp of his time will seize the language of the day to rework the pieces into a convincing tapestry of meaning. The outcome is sometimes the patched quilt of a *Wasteland* or a woven carpet of a *Ulysses*. The readers of myths, the decoders of the palimpsest, must necessarily decipher myths to unravel cryptic layers of meaning. Thereby hangs a plan for the contemporary reader.

In the 18th century, Hegel philosophised on history, which is itself a philosopher's effort to enlighten modern man about historical evolution intellectually. But one can also see Hegels' *Philosophy of History* as weaving the German idealist's myth about the cunning of reason evolving from primitive barbaric tribes with limited freedom to modern Christian nations-as-states where people are free to act in their interest as well as the interest of the collective consciousness. Lévi-Strauss, for instance, would take exception to the Hegelian labelling of 'pre-historic' communities as primitive. He would rather address them as 'primitive' communities that never felt the need, nor possessed the bourgeois luxury to write their history.

In 1949, Mircea Eliade wrote *The Myth of the Eternal Return*, a philosophy of history that was different from the Hegelian argument. He, however, added the subtitle *Cosmos and History* as an unintended counterpoint to Hegel. In his more humane approach to *The Myth of the Eternal Return* (1949), he formulates the most fundamental concept: an enlightened distinction between "archaic" man and "modern" man. This distinction is better understood as two radically opposed attitudes to history and time. The archaic man is traditionally disposed to see history paradigmatically. To him, life evolves from paradigm to paradigm as a set of recurring patterns that carries symbolic meaning. This renders 'archaic' or 'primitive' man more metahistorical, in that he carves out of history a transcendental meaning.

In clear contrast to the primitive man is the "modern" man who finds himself trapped in a more concrete time with a sense of drifting and falling off the precipice. This recurring motif of having to get a hold on things is echoed by T.S Eliot in "Marie, Marie, Hold on Tight!" The poem depicts modern man as alienated from his own time. This means that uprooted modern man must submit himself to a Hegelian deterministic scheme in which even Napolean or Joan of Arc are instruments of history's autonomous cunning of reason.

Archaic man trusted the integrity of his symbols and archetypes to see himself inhabiting a much larger space, beyond the bounds of history. Archaic man saw himself making meaning out of a cosmic existence. Modern man, bruised by Enlightenment, still kept the Cartesian sword of doubt as the chief weapon to thrust, penetrate and cut through the confusions of his times in the world. The sword of doubt, which is also the sword of reason, first severed modern man's contact with the cosmos. Archetypes were released from functional memory as if they were a remedy to a traditional way of life. But the released archetypes did not run into oblivion, thanks to the modern writer's determination to restore them to history. The consolation that the modern writer provides is that even though we may not recover a lost cosmos, we will still be able to recover our lost history and a lost world. Only that we must tell the stories differently by repurposing the signs and filling the signifiers with contemporary motivation.

The present collection of articles brings together writers and academics who have approached myth as a rich resource for retelling stories, reworking the perennial possibilities of telling the same story from an unlikely perspective, and of reading the many motivations that lie in the myth's subterranean regions. Anand Neelakantan and Anuja Chandramouli are established writers who render voice to mythological characters who have been demonised, reviled, and misunderstood. In an age in which digital visualisation has only stoked the appetite for wonder, these writers feed the popular imagination with their perspectival reworkings of mythological tales. In the first section, the author-speak by Anand Neelakantan and Anuja Chandramouli offers valuable insights that almost lay bare the technique of turning age-old narratives into timeless retellings. There is an anticipation that accompanies an author's confession; it is the expectation that some secret about weaving a mythological yarn will tumble out.

Swarnalatha Rangarajan and A. V. Koshy are academics who are also creative writers. Their works bear powerful messages for humanity as they celebrate the import of myth in a baffling cosmos. Swarnalatha's is the longest piece on the irrepressible Sita. Her quiet and serene telling of tense moments of the *Ramayana* offers yet another version of Sita – a *Sitayana*. Koshy's passion for poetry and Greek mythology finds form in the lament for Hector.

The Editor's Workshop focuses on how to analyse mythical texts from various viewpoints. Lakshmi Krishna Kumar's article on *The Penelopiad* is used as an example to offer hints on writing a research paper. Further, the creative texts of Swarnalatha and Koshy serve as ideal examples to demonstrate how a text can be analysed and interpreted.

The section titled The Critic/ Researcher contains research articles by Sujatha Menon, A. R. Chitra, Anjitha Anil and Sushant Kishore, which are fine demonstrations of myth criticism. Sujatha Menon's essay offers clear insights on the concept of myth and mythopoeia and is one that will truly benefit researchers of myth. Chitra's article deals with the nature of mythmaking in Roshani Chokshi's *Star-Touched Stories*. Anjitha's and Sushant's article focuses on the portrayal of Ahalya in Kane's novel, *Ahalya's Awakening*.

The last section, Book Reports/ Reviews, is in keeping with the theme of the book. Fr. Joby's book report on Robert Segal's book is essential for a deep understanding of myth. This is followed by reviews of the latest mythopoeic fiction – Durga's and Barathi's review of Neelakantan's *Nala Damayanti* (2023) and Yuvaraj's review of Haynes' *Stone Blind* (2022). I can see the ageless Northrop Frye, that sage of Archetypal Criticism, nod approval.

Vinod Balakrishnan, Professor of English, Department of Humanities and Social Sciences, National Institute of Technology, Tiruchirappalli, is a practising poet, motivational speaker, reviewer of books and a yoga enthusiast. He is the General Editor of the 12-volume **Encyclopaedia of World Mythology (2013)** *in Malayalam. He has coauthored* **Politickle Lines: Conversations with Indian Political Cartoonists (2018), Somaesthetics and Yogasutra (2020),** *and* **The Language of Humour and its Transmutation in Indian Political Cartoons (2023)**. *His research interests include Somaesthetics, Politics of Representation, Film Studies, Life Writing and Narratives about India.*

The Artefact and the Artisan

Myth, Culture, and Women in India

Anand Neelakantan

Anand Neelakantan is one of India's top-selling authors. He has thirteen books to his credit and his writings are mostly revisionist renderings. His debut novel, **Asura: Tale of the Vanquished (2012)**, *presents the* **Ramayana** *from the antagonist Ravana's perspective. His* **Bahubali Trilogy (2017-2020)** *which serves as a prequel to the Bahubali movie is one of his most reputed writings. Neelakantan was the recipient of the Kalinga International Literary Award in 2017. His latest novel,* **Nala Damayanti (2023)**, *has been reviewed in this book. Another of his latest works,* **Mahi: The Elephant Who Flew Over the Blue Mountains (2023)**, *crafted for children and young adults, is intended to be an Indian* **Jungle Book** *.*

Bhakti literature based on devotion towards a personal god has made a major contribution to Indian culture in the form of mellifluous poetry, devotional songs, temple dance forms, classical music and architecture. However, the Bhakti movement also marked the end of debate and discussion in Indian thought. One major ill effect of this was the diminishing independence and freedom of women in society.

There is a marked difference in the way women characters are depicted in epic, classical and medieval literature. Most of what passes for culture and middle-class ethical values belong to the medieval era. Either women became an impediment to men's spiritual progress or they were relegated to the inner courtyards of joint families and burdened with the responsibility of carrying the yoke of tradition on their shoulders. *Adarsh Naari* or the model woman was the one who obeyed her husband slavishly.

If we go by the sculptures and paintings of ancient India, we find women and men intermingling in society with equal freedom. Even the dresses they wear are similar, with no upper garments. Also, we see women without covering their faces or heads.

The repeated invasions and subjugation in the Gangetic plains changed Indian culture and its treatment of women. This era, which coincided with the rise of the Bhakti movement, forced women to wear veils, and cover their heads, and in doing so, relegated them to the darkness of inner courtyards. This cultural change is reflected in the characterisation of women in our Puranas. The Sita of *Tulsidas Ramayan* is not the Sita of Valmiki's. Tulsidas' *Ramacharitamanas*, a product of its time and geography, played an important part in shaping the image of Sita as a demure, obedient, weak woman who needs a husband to protect her. Sita eventually became deified as the *Aadarsh Naari*.

Sita is an Aadarsh Naari for Valmiki too but for entirely different reasons. It is Sita's choices that provide the impetus to the plot of Ramayana. When Rama asks her to stay back in Ayodhya instead of accompanying him to the forest, she refuses to do so. She refuses to be confined to the Lakshmana Rekha and steps out to give alms to the mendicant, as that is her dharma. When Hanuman offers to rescue her from Ashoka Vana, she refuses to be rescued and says, it is Rama's dharma to rescue her. Sita volunteers for *Agnipariksha* in Lanka and it isn't Rama who asks for it. It is her choice.

Later, when Rama abandons her, fearing scandal, Sita refuses to give up. She brings up her sons, acts as their guru and trains them so well that they vanquish the entire army of Ayodhya. When Rama asks for a trial by fire before accepting her again, Sita chooses to go back to the womb of Mother Earth. None of the above indicates a demure, helpless damsel who needs a man to rescue her. She is the master of her own life, the creator of her own destiny.

Unlike Draupadi who gets pawned, stripped, humiliated and has to depend on her husbands to avenge her honour, Sita goes through life with confidence and self-assurance. This is precisely why Sita is an Adarsh Naari, not because she is a shadow of Rama. The shy, docile, teary-eyed Sita is a creation of a television series based on the medieval Ramayanas. Not just Sita, but all the women of *Valmiki Ramayana* are confident and not dependent on the men of their lives. Whether it is Meenakshi, better known as Soorpanakha, the sister of Ravana, or Shanta, the little-known elder sister of Rama, Valmiki's women characters possess a certain depth of character. But to analyse such characters, we must view these myths afresh and not bind them to the conventional and popular male-centric narratives.

Devotional or Bhakti literature, which was written with a specific purpose, has its unique place in the realm of myth. But like most myths, many of its narratives may be construed as unpalatable in the present day. However, this is not the case with all. For instance, the *Valmiki Ramayana* appears more modern in its treatment of women characters. My book *Valmiki's Women* is an attempt to explore Ramayana through the eyes of marginal characters like Soorpanakha, Shanta, Manthara and Tataka.

Mythology and Me

Anuja Chandramouli

Anuja Chandramouli is a bestselling author and new-age Indian classicist widely regarded as one of the finest writers in mythology, historical fiction and fantasy. Her debut novel was **Arjuna: Saga of a Pandava Warrior-Prince** *(2012).* Some of her other books include **Kartikeya: The Destroyer's Son (2017), Prithviraj Chauhan: The Emperor of Hearts (2017),** and **Ganga: The Constant Goddess (2018).** *Her book,* **Mohini: The Enchantress (2020)** *was the winner of the JK Papers and Times of India Popular Choice Author award for the year 2021.* **Abhimanyu: Son of Arjuna (2022)** *is her latest novel.*

People think writing books on mythology is easy. Hell, in fact, most who don't know better assume that penning a novel itself is one of those cushy jobs, where you sit your butt down, hammer a few keys, pause for long breaks where you chug coffee by the gallon while staring aimlessly into the distance pretending to be busy, and out pops a finished manuscript, but that is a rant for another day.

Getting back to the prior point, the general assumption seems to be that all one needs to be a successful author nowadays is to choose any character from mythology, brush up on the tales grandma used to narrate and reproduce it as best as can be managed. This means plugging the gaps in memory with artistic license designed to generate as much outrage as possible. In other words, you calibrate it to that fine point Chetan Bhagat has perfected where you get to laugh all the way to the bank having managed to manufacture a viral response without incurring the wrath of the *bhakts* (devotees) who may just be inclined to bomb you into oblivion for taking liberties with our 'rich cultural heritage.'

I have lost track of the number of people who have congratulated me on my brilliant decision to take up this cash cow which has the added benefit of being sacred and milking it for all it's worth in the current political climate where it is practically a mandate that we revere all things bovine. Needless to say, this is the sort of thing which makes one empathise with those entitled, privileged celeb kids who spit fire every time they hear the word nepotism, insisting that they had to slog it out to make their mark in a cruel, unforgiving industry that treats everybody just the same, irrespective of gender and pedigree.

The truth is, writing about Indian mythology is like walking on a tightrope across a massive gorge without a safety harness. Or a life vest. Or even a cable for that matter. The material is delicate and volatile which is why solid, painstaking research work is a must since it is the only thing that makes for an adequate safety net. During the inevitable plunge into the depths, it is the only thing that can facilitate a bounce back or prevent one attempting the Herculean task from going splat.

Needless to say, I recommend thoroughness or an intimate familiarity with Puranic lore most strongly.

It is important to treat the source material with the respect it deserves given that Indian mythology is a treasure trove that keeps on giving. Within its fathomless depths lie the solution to every conundrum, keys to knowledge, precious insight into universal truths and answers to every question that has ever been asked or will be, irrespective of whether it is profane or profound. Mining into its core will yield not only pearls of wisdom but forkfuls of folly, both of which are equally informative when used to apprise the life choices that fall to us to make. There are silly parables to entertain children and complex philosophies to confound Confucius. The information gleaned could mean everything, anything, and nothing.

That said though, slavish parroting of the stories contained therein is a foolhardy attempt since nothing is set in stone. Ours was originally an oral tradition, all the better to preserve the entirely organic and assimilative quality of this ever-shape-shifting entity called Mythology. Every story has many variations and even more permutations are happening even as this is being typed out, in the hands of myth makers and new-age storytellers.

This constant metamorphosis is most welcome, especially when coloured with unique shades of perspective that imbue the older versions with fresh layers and multiple hues that make it all the more glorious, relevant and thought-provoking. This fluidity is the main factor that has ensured the survival of our myths and aided in the preservation of its innate charm. Therefore it must not only be tolerated but perpetuated and actively encouraged.

Perhaps in trying to establish that writing on Indian mythology is daredevilry at its most dangerous which involves a delicate balancing act between maintaining the integrity of the core while building upon it, taking in the requirements of the age in which it is set. I have oversold my case and made it all sound risky, too extreme (if such a thing were possible) and tedious, best suited for the closet rebels among the pedagogues. When it comes to the unvarnished truth though, mythology is endlessly fascinating and loads of fun!

As far as I am concerned, Indian mythology and writing about it never gets old. Ever. There is always the prospect of exploration, adventure and fresh discovery. It has the feeling of easy intimacy shared only with the oldest of friends who have been a part of your life forever, while holding out the chance to make new ones who may just grab your hand and take you on a rollicking ride that may just turn out to be the experience of a lifetime.

For me, the lifelong affair with mythology has been one hell of an incredible romance. It has been a captivating journey that has taught me everything that went on to shape my identity personally and professionally while taking me to wonderful places and helping me meet lovely people. Forevermore, I will remain grateful for the magic and wonder, the blessing that Indian mythology has infused my life with. It is my fondest hope and strongest belief that this love story will last forever. And a day.

Sita's Hypothesis

Swarnalatha Rangarajan

Swarnalatha Rangarajan, Professor of English, Department of Humanities and Social Sciences, IIT Madras, is passionate about environmental humanities. She is the founding editor of the **Indian Journal of Ecocriticism** *(IJE) and a guest editor for* **The Trumpeter***, the flagship journal of the deep ecology movement. She has many academic publications to her credit, the latest being* **Handbook of Medical-Environmental Humanities (2022)** *and* **Literary Desertscapes in the Global South and Beyond: Anthropocene Naturecultures (2023)***. She has also penned short fiction dealing with women, myth, and the environment.*

The solitary Ashoka tree in the scorched *vana* jabbered away to Sita who listened patiently with her arms wrapped around its trunk. The ancestral voices of the surrounding forests joined the tree's dirge.

From afar the deep-throated waves of Sethusamudram emitted a guttural chant, all out-breath. Tuning in to the mood of the reckless ocean, Sita could sense earthquakes in its dark belly that were waiting to manifest and tip the balance. The sea's angry rumble did not augur well for events waiting to manifest in its indigo depths. The giant waves kept up their frenetic chorus. "Not a blade of grass will remain! Everything will be on fire!" They repeated these words again and again until the cautionary message entered the collective psyche of the five elements.

It was midnight and the night wanderers, the *nishachara*, paid their obeisance to Sita and quickly passed by without disturbing her. The night was warm, warmer than it should be at that time of the year. Sita noticed that the leaves of the Ashoka tree were not willing to open their stomata. The night air was heavy with noxious exhalations, the odours of charred vegetation and rotting human flesh from the battlefields where Rama and his army were battling the *asura* hordes of the obstinate Ravana.

Sita caressed the tree with her long, slender fingers in an attempt to calm the cascading waves of agony that the tree was emitting through its strong kinaesthetic field. She understood the emotion. It was a collective fear channelled from the voices of the wilderness in the surrounding hills and forests.

Sita closed her eyes and meditated. The inevitable would anyway happen. The coronation at Ayodhya and the panorama of happy reunions of wife with husband, mothers with sons and brother with brother were all foregone conclusions which did not interest her. In her mind's eye, she saw a barren, lunar landscape where the five elements had withdrawn their creative potential. The blue-hued Rama would reach for the *Brahmastra* when he found Ravana's severed heads growing back in a hydra-like fashion.

The mighty weapon would blaze forth with the luminosity of a thousand suns creating a landscape of erasure. However the drama would not end at that point since this was not the real climax – the decisive battle between good and evil, polarised as Rama and Ravana, sung and celebrated by future generations of humans in epic grandeur as the *Ramayana*.

Even the lotus-eyed Rama was not aware of what lay beyond the immediate battlefields of Lanka. The true horror would descend after Rama's sleep was ushered in by the hurricane blast arrow of the Lord of Lanka. While the avatar slept, centuries would roll forward bringing to the forefront the powerful monster with a hundred heads - the Shatakanta Ravana. And she, as *Prakriti*, the material cause of the earth, would be forced to respond.

Sita wondered if the bards would record this twist in the epic and devote a chapter to Sita's intervention. Would the epic be called a *Sitayana* which would record her struggle to maintain a sense of balance? She had been through these ordeals as long as she could remember, defining and redefining the material conditions needed for survival on the planet.

Sita shuddered at the recollection of Indrajit's deadly *astra* employed on the battlefield a few days ago. Future generations would invent a new name for it – radioactivity. Its dull green fire shrouded the earth for many miles extending beyond the battlefield before it targeted Lakshmana. Rama had thrown away his weapons in grief. The loyal Hanuman promptly abducted Ravana's physician, Sushena, to extract the secret of the life-reviving Sanjeevini herb from him. However, when Hanuman arrived in the fragrant Valley of the Flowers, the herb refused to reveal itself to him. Its plant spirit, cool to the touch like watery jade, appeared before Sita pleading for the boon of invisibility.

"Your dharma is to heal, O Sanjeevini. Then why do you go against your innate nature?" Sita had wonderingly asked the herb, marvelling at the way its presence was rejuvenating the Ashoka *vana*.

"I speak not in selfishness or an attitude of denial, mother. If the humans learn the secret of my innermost essence, they will use it for their own contorted ends. Mother Ritambari, the keeper of all harmony, you must know this!" The plant spirit continued, "They will patent my *jiva*, extract my innards and meddle with my genetic coding. The rich and famous among them who can afford to buy me will live for a longer duration and chase the dream of immortality."

Sita closed her eyes and reflected; the plant spirit was speaking the truth. Sita saw strangulated water bodies and denuded forests giving way to a barren, blasted urban wilderness. A new avatar of *rakshasas* roamed the earth exercising a powerful grid of control. These transgenic humanoids would colonise the earth like a swarm of locusts and secure their longevity in ugly, climate-controlled, steel citadels.

She smiled wearily at the plant spirit and said, "Your wish will be granted but fate has decreed you to play your role in the battlefield. You cannot escape from that!" And true to her promise, the eagle-eyed Hanuman went blind while searching for the plant in the midst of the riot of colours in the Valley of Flowers. He closed his eyes and meditated on Rama. The solution to the problem came to him in a flash, as swift as a *rama bana*, an arrow from Rama's bow. He uprooted the entire Dronagiri mountain and headed towards Lanka without for a moment noticing the gaping crater-like hole he had made in the febrile Himalayan terrain. Leaning against the Ashoka tree, Sita witnessed the scene and fore suffered it all. Hanuman had set a new trend.

The tree had become a close friend ever since Ravana imprisoned her in the Ashoka Vana, which in the good old days had been a leafy retreat resonant with the morning songs of *Krauncha* birds. The salubrious garden on the mountaintop in which Ravana had imprisoned her had now been reduced to a dull brown patch of earth with a few trees that bravely resisted the onslaught of the raging war. The profuse *rama bana* flowers with their blood red blossoms had also disappeared.

Ravana's maidservants had wondered long at the exotic blooms which magically sprung up when Sita set foot in the *vana*. Looking at the configuration of petals, stamens and pistils that resembled a human being carrying a bow, they cried out, "Look don't these flowers resemble her husband, Sri Rama?" They unanimously conferred the title, "Rama's bow" on the exuberant blooms.

The tree brought her news from the world of humans and nature. She would listen very carefully to these little narratives coming from the tree because the authors and contributors were often other-than-humans. It was only the other day that the tree gave her the deer's version of the story of Sita's abduction.

"I wonder why Mother Sita allowed that poltroon of a Ravana to carry her away! She duped the world into thinking that she is an ordinary woman easily enamoured by trivial things like a golden deer. She also gave us a bad name. After the epic is written, deer will always go down in human history as vain creatures who lead virtuous women astray. We will become the favourite targets of hunters who are already ill-disposed towards us."

Sita would wince as she listened to these narratives. These gentle creatures had an insight into her true identity. The deer was right. There was no logical explanation for the unfolding web of events. The stage was already set and the sky father gods requested her to step into the allotted role. She had tried reasoning with them but they gave her a catalogue of reasons to choose from! Old karmic links, thoughtless boons granted by male gods, the secret mission of avatars, and evolution arising from the purification of the earth-bound life. It was a long list and Sita grew tired of following the logic. "Leave me out of all this!" she had cried, raising her hands in mock supplication.

They smiled at her and said, "Man's destiny is bound to the earth's. The gods who come down to the earth are not exempt from it. You wield the axle of dharma! Ritambari, you are the underlying order - the warp and weft of this universe. When you are the accommodating space of all that happens on earth, how can you ever think of excusing yourself from all its drama? Moreover, the ending will be happy. It will usher in an era of prosperity and development for men and women in the golden era of Rama's rule, the *Rama rajya*!"

Sita had chosen not to respond to this tall talk. As she disappeared into the hammered golden light of the fading dusk, a sky god called out mischievously, "The rain will fall regularly in the land of Rama. Now that should make you happy!" Sita knew that it was time to assume a human form and enter limiting human time. She preferred being in the deep time of mountains and rivers in which the world was created afresh every moment.

Embodied in a human form, Sita felt trapped in a world that was not created spontaneously like the silent lotus of incomparable beauty growing from the navel of the divine dreamer. It was a world of strange miscegenations fashioned by human demiurges who no longer believed in the quest for wholeness. As Shatakantha Ravana would later point out to her with a swagger, "Prakriti, you are dead or altered beyond recognition! You are not hidden so you do not need to be unveiled. Goddess no more, you are only a construction, movement and displacement. You are no longer the primordial mother, the dream of oneness, the teeming womb of the universe, the matrix, origin or the perennial site for replenishment."

But she couldn't let things fall apart. The Sky Gods were right, everything was hers. There was absolutely nothing to let go of. It was an amusing thought. A gentle, prayerful voice interrupted her reverie. "Mother! You know your power. How can you allow this to happen?" Sita didn't quite know how to handle the question. The old woman kneeling near the trunk of the Ashoka tree quivered with the intensity of her question. "Goddess!" she cried out, "I recognized you from afar. These demonesses who guard this sacred grove are stupid! Don't they know that they are trying to imprison one who is as free as the wind?"

Sita kept her silence. After all, today was Vijayadashami, the day when Rama was destined to self-actualise his epic role. She had to wait in patience till the moment summoned her. She gathered her long flowing tresses into a tight knot and buried her face in her knees pretending to drop into slumber.

"Goddess!" the persistent voice did not allow her to sleep. Sita lifted her head and took a close look at the woman. Though crisscrossed by a hundred wrinkles, her face shone like polished ebony. She was surely a tribal from the neighbouring hills. But someone clearly distinguished! It was not the impressive gold loop that she wore as a nose ring that caught Sita's eye but the clear eyes that glistened like precious gems in her furrowed face.

She continued in her throbbing voice, "You are the force in the wind, the wetness in water, the heat in the fire, the quickening of life in the soil, the vastness of space. How can you allow yourself to be imprisoned by these nitwits who don't recognise you?"

Sita recognised her. It was Shabari, the Bhil ascetic, who plucked and tasted plum after plum before offering them to her beloved Sri Rama. Sita hushed her and stole a nervous glance at Ravana's female dakinis specially hired to guard the Ashoka vana. Luckily they were lost to the world. There had been a generous flow of strong liquors and good food after the bloody battle yesterday.

Sita beckoned the old woman to her stony seat. "What brings you here to Ravana's harsh kingdom, O wise mother!? Have you come to have a darshan of your beloved Sri Rama?" Shabari fell silent for a moment and then asked, "When the child is in distress, whom does it go running to seeking solace?"

Sita gazed into the eyes of the old woman, as limpid as the waters of the Manasarovar lake in the early hours of the *Brahma muhurta*. She knew why Shabari had come. In those calm patient eyes, Sita saw the agony of an entire community pushed to the fringes of civilisation.

The old woman continued, "We gave our lands to water their cities. Now they have destroyed our homes. We have nowhere to go. Our forests are gone. They set fire to them to build their cities. We have become orphans! Will all this be set right after the grand moment when my Lord Sri Rama will take you back to Ayodhya in a triumphant procession?" Sita patted the old woman affectionately and said, "All in good time, wise mother! There will be a new earth for you to rejoice in."

Shabari trembled like a withered leaf and asked, "Is there going to be a *Maha pralaya*? I can feel it in my bones. The new earth that you speak of can come only after a great deluge which will wash away the corruptions that fester on this earth?" Sita replied with a smile, "You speak of the cleansing amniotic waters of life, wise mother Shabari! But the titillating part of the Ramayana story is always the test of fire – the *agni pariksha*." Sita's face lit up with an inner fire as she uttered these words.

Shabari folded her hands and said, "Goddess, the past, present and future of the trichiliocosms cannot be concealed from you. Forgive Sri Rama for what he is going to demand from you. The God of Fire will hang his head with shame for having to witness you entering his holy flames!"

Sita laughed again. Shabari for a moment imagined that she saw a pair of dhamshtra, sharp fangs where pearly teeth should be. Sita's voice grew deep as she said, "Wise mother Shabari, the event you predict is the second Agnipariksha. The one I speak comes prior to that and is more exacting; it is a test in which I will have to delve deep into the poison fires to quench them. The bards in times to come will conveniently ignore this ordeal by fire."

Shabari's face wore an expression of deep understanding as she knelt down before Sita and said, "Please allow me to be by your side when this happens." "So be it!" said Sita as she set about preparing herself for the events of the day. She sat cross-legged, her fingers touching the earth in a *bhu sparsha* mudra. She offered a silent prayer to the divinity within her, burning like a flame. Closing her eyes, she told Shabari, "I have a lot of samskaras to burn before I meet Ravana. I am going into a *yoga nidra*. Hanuman will come here during the course of the day bringing the news that Rama is wounded on the battlefield. Tap me gently on my right shoulder, wise mother and do not be afraid to find me in altered form."

Sita leaned against the Ashoka tree and plunged into the depths of her ancient, primordial mind. To Shabari she appeared asleep but Sita's consciousness hovered around the razor-sharp state of deep awareness. The sacred syllable on which she meditated took her through the contracting and expanding loops of the earth's history in the last four and a half year billion years of evolution.

Maid, mother and crone - Sita beheld the triple goddesses' reflection in the clear waters of her mind. The changing kaleidoscope revealed her youthful body, ethereal and gaseous, that was enveloped in the radiant energy of the celestial bodies, distant stars and cosmic winds; the pattern changed to reveal a nebulous beauty gradually solidifying into the solid, green nurturing lap of the dazzling, diverse earth sangha; the pattern soon reorganised itself, changing colour and form to become dry cupreous earth battered by deluging oceans and storm surges.

As she gazed deeper, Sita found these reflections blurring and throwing up a free vortex of whirring images – her original face. She watched with terrified fascination the panoramic play of evolution, whose essence was the bubbling karmic cocktail of life which oozed, mutated and spilled over in perpetual motion. The sacred *pranava* enveloped everything in this passionate play. The play which was authored in both comic and tragic modes had actors from the council of all beings ranging from stardust to cyborgs. And she as director, had issued cue cards to mark the entrances and exits of innumerable births, mass extinctions, rebirths, catastrophes and other perennial becomings. She saw her own fruiting, evolving, decaying body with passionate dispassion and saluted her essence that flowed through bodied life forms uninterruptedly as the vital mystery of life. Sita arrived at a deep luminous calm in the midst of the spinning inner vortex where there was no fear.

She opened her eyes when she felt Shabari's gentle tap on her shoulder. Her eyes first fell upon Hanuman's puzzled face. He stood in his customary bent position, with tail lassoing the sun and hands folded in salutation but there was bewilderment in his eyes. Shabari looked more composed; Sita noticed that she was chanting a hymn to Kali. "How is my lord?" asked Sita springing up her seat with a warrior-like gait.

Hanuman's eyes brimmed with tears as he reported the events of the day in a choked voice, "My lord Sri Rama was struck unconscious by Ravana's evil *astra*. The valiant Lakshmana is paralysed. There is chaos on the battlefield. Ravana has gone into hiding and his elder brother, the monstrous Shatakanta Ravana, has taken charge. Nobody knows how to deal with him. He is neither a demon nor a human being. His body glints like burnished gold and his energy is indefatigable. Even the *rakshasas* give him a wide berth. His weapons are mighty, they say. Once directed towards their targets, they become hurricanes of fire and scorch everything around for miles and miles. The rumours are that…"

Sita raised her hand and bade Hanuman to stop. "The fear I detect in your voice does not become you, O son of the wind! Even if the Ravana you speak of is Kalki the destroyer himself, I want to have an audience with him. Lead me to him!"

Hanuman fell on his knees and said, "Mother! Forgive this humble servant. My brains are addled and the strangeness of the world in which I find myself makes me behave in strange ways. But tell me this divine mother. Why do you look so fierce and why have you taken on this terrible form discarding all your beauty? I have often heard my Lord Sri Rama say that your beauty is superior to the idea of beauty itself. The reason poets in the country have run out of their stock of similes while attempting to describe you. Gentle mother, your compassionate face as gentle and fair as the *sharad* moon, why does it blaze in anger like a meteor? Your lotus-like eyes always demure and full of compassion, why are they bloodshot? Your bejewelled tresses, braided and coiled like the holy Adishesha on whom my lord rests in his ocean kingdom, are now let loose like a sheet of torrential rain. Your skin as soft and radiant as a *kimsuka* flower has become scaly and dark in hue. You appear to be the formidable Kali who dances her dread dance of creation in the glow of the burning corpses, creating life afresh from things that decay and rot. Who are you, divine Mother? You appear to be my mother Sita and at the same time you appear not to be her!"

Sita raised her hand to put an end to Hanuman's impassioned musings and proclaimed, "Don't bind me with the strangle rope of duality, Hanuman. Lead me to the battlefield." The battlefield resembled a still life painting. The air was heavy with the stench of death. A wake of rapacious vultures swooped down to inspect the mortalities but refused to eat the decaying flesh. Rama's body was unscarred and it appeared that he was in a deep sleep. Loyal Lakshmana lay at his feet, his limbs frozen in a strange paralysis. Ravana's asura hordes had also fled the battlefield. The heavy brooding silence in the surrounding sentinel-like hills was complemented by the heaving gong-like clamour of the sea. Sita moved in silence followed by Shabari and Hanuman, utterly unmindful of the terrifying carnage all around.

Shortly there was a metallic whirring of wings and the smog-covered firmament parted to reveal a shining bronze citadel-like structure gravitating towards the battlefield with great speed. "The war is going to begin and Ravana will appreciate meeting me alone. Why don't both of you take refuge in that enclave near the rampart and watch the proceedings?" said Sita feeling the rush of adrenaline in her veins.

The citadel on wheels was trying to land. Sita started walking toward it and was greeted by a shower of arrows disgorged from a tiny aperture in its gleaming structure. Hanuman roared with anger and would have pounced on the unseen bowman but for Shabari's restraining hand.

"Remove the notion that your Mother Sita has to be protected. Can't you see that she revels in putting on disguises? Now she has taken her original cosmic form to fight the war with Ravana, who is again only an appearance. When she is the raw clay out of which everything is baked in this earth, can there be any question of winning or subduing her, O son of the Wind?" Realising the wisdom in Shabari's words, Hanuman restrained himself.

The continuous shower of arrows caused rivulets of blood to flow from Sita's dark-hued body. Laughing boisterously she advanced towards the enemy her large, defiant eyes whirring in circles. Bellowing loud, she stripped the corpses of their flesh and made a garland for herself out of the skulls. The bones, she picked clean and fashioned them into anklets. Her harsh laughter reverberated fearsomely in all directions. With lolling tongue she shook the blood droplets dripping from her arm and the moment they touched the earth they became *rakta bijikas*, seeds of blood which spawned innumerable other copies of her dread form. The *bijikas* roamed the battlefield feeding on the mortalities left untouched by the vultures. The field was wiped clean in a matter of seconds. Sita laughed again. Her voice was as aggressive as the ocean at the time of *Pralaya*.

The door of the citadel opened and Ravana emerged carefully making sure that his hundred heads were not unduly traumatised while crawling out of the narrow exit door. Ravana looked human. His powerful muscular body was devoid of any armour plate. He stood tall at eight feet and focused his hundred pairs of eyes unblinkingly at Sita. There was no anger, no rapaciousness or combustive emotions lurking in those depths.

"What brings you here, Ravana?" thundered Sita preparing herself for the final onslaught. Ravana stretched himself and advanced a couple of steps with a steady gait. He addressed Sita in a deep metallic timbre, "Sita in costume dress! Cut the crap, lady! You can't scare me with your show of blood and gore. I don't know fear. Even if you want to convince me that you are a goddess you will fail because I don't understand what devotion is. Can't figure out what it is to tremble with fear and awe before the holy of holies. Or if you think I am kinky and will be turned on by a woman with blood-stained fangs, there too you don't score a point, because I don't need women. I don't have sex instincts. Well, you must wonder as to what brought us together. Well, it is business! Let us talk business. I need you—to be more specific, your resources, not the sundry baubles that you have but precious stuff like thorium and uranium - the crown jewels of your treasure chest. Treasures you have tucked away from my panoptic surveillance by the sheer virtue of your illusory powers that hide and camouflage the material of your gross world. I need to grasp your few remaining mysteries. I need to ravish you, lady!"

Sita set aside her anger and looked intently at the young man in front of her. It was difficult to brand him evil since he didn't have a concept of dharma. As distant and icy as the comets, he was a creature of vacuum bored with the outmoded paradigms of good and evil. She had come ready to slay a demon but this creature didn't deserve the honour of that rite. Ravana nodded his hundred heads in affirmation. He had tapped into her field of mental energy and knew what she was thinking.

"That's right lady!" he said, "Don't waste time in trying to kill me. I am a telomerase miracle. My cells will never grow old and moreover, my genome mapping is so perfect that my body can never be subjected to decay like the putrid flesh of these poor critters lying all around. I am no kin to that old dotard, Ravana who lusts after you."

"Then why are you here, O hundred-headed monster?" demanded Sita baring her fangs. "It is a matter of sheer convenience lady. And mind you, don't call me a hundred-headed monster. My hundred heads can process, store and weave in information pertaining to several galaxies. My sudden entry into your archaic time was spurred by the sudden serendipitous retrieval of one precious nugget of information sitting inside an optical jukebox which was connected to my sixty-ninth central processing cranial unit. And yes, although I cannot feel emotions, I felt an unrecognised drive in me to see you who is considered to be the master fictive construct of our times- the primordial mother whose milk nourished our ancestor races who were free from genetic tinkering. Perhaps it was all about seeing you as an interactive mirror, as an ambiguous Other against which I both recognise and measure myself."

Sita chuckled and said, "You are in the infancy of consciousness, O Ravana! Bounded in your monadic illusion of separateness you forget that you are one in essence with me. Like the millions of creatures who have sprung from my lap, you too are a holograph of the universe with my maternal signature etched on your core. Your genetically altered being is nothing but a new wave which breaks on the shores of manifestation; the ocean remains ever itself."

Ravana's response was brusque and minimal. "You forget that the self-replicating cells in my body were generated by computers. You can be no mother, midwife or wet nurse to hyper-evolved beings like me. I am running short of time. You have an hour to willingly submit yourself to my probes. If not, I am afraid I will have to use my sophisticated weapons which will scorch everything on this land in a nearly 2000-degrees-Fahrenheit flame. You will die, and so will your so-called two million-plus species. As for me, I have acquired lifespan escape velocity. My lightning-swift citadel is immune to all frailties of your flesh and it can transport me to a distant planet which I can colonise and mould according to my needs."

Before Ravana could complete reciting from his inventory of threats, a bolt of lightning descended like Indra's vajra setting the entire landscape on fire. Ravana did some quick computations and the powerful geo-surveillance optoelectronic rods embedded in his heads alerted him to the situation. "Lady, you are finished!" he proclaimed without excitement or trepidation, "Underwater Methyl hydrate has been ignited. Triggered by volcanic activity in the ocean bed. More than 100,000 trillion cubic feet of this gas has been released. Your all-too-human children are to be blamed for this. They have been pushing the buttons over the centuries. This gas will raise the planet's temperature by at least 13 degrees Fahrenheit, according to my calculations. So in addition to fires, you will have floods due to ice caps melting. Messy scenario! Isn't it? The time has come when you can prove to me now that you are the essence. Step into these hellish fires and quench them. If you do so, I will acknowledge you as the sole creatrix and magna mater."

The hungry flames were fast devouring everything. Sita knew that it was time to act. She gave the unperturbed Ravana a piercing look and quietly asked, "Are you challenging me to undergo a test of fire?" The demon laughed and mirthless tears rolled down his hundred cheeks. "I am dead serious! But for the fact that I can never be dead," he said enjoying his wordplay.

Sita summoned the seven-tongued Agni, who rose from the waters of the seething cauldron of the Sethusamudram. The Rig Vedic seer who named him the "grandson of the waters" – Aapam Napat, after witnessing flames which surfaced from oil seepages in water was prophetic.

Red-faced Agni who was seated in his bejewelled chariot had the cold detached look of an executioner. The fiery horses that yoked his chariot revelled in the uncontrolled dance of flames that enveloped the whole place. "Why did you summon me, O Prakriti? Don't you behold my divine design in these calamities that will summon this earth to its end?

"O Chosen priest of the gods, oblation bearer, radiant one, dispeller of darkness, is it not your dharma to protect this earth?" asked Sita, her face all ablaze with anger. "O daughter of Janaka, don't you recognize that I come as a destroyer at this point in your history when everything has come full circle? In these times of pralaya, even water takes on my dread form and destruction becomes my dharma. So don't expect me to rescue you or furnish a testimony for your nurturing powers!"

Sita's dark-hued face took on the hard brilliance of a diamond. Her voice rose above the hiss of the sulphurous ocean and the crackling of the wavelets of fire. "O vain god of Fire! Apocalyptic scenarios don't threaten my imagination. Know me as the regulatory force of this universe. Know that I have maintained the temperature on this earth's surface for hundreds of millions of yugas despite Surya increasing his heat and the *vayu mandala* changing its composition. Know that I am the force that stabilises the salinity in the great oceans. If I had allowed the salt concentration to rise, the seas would have long been emptied of life. If I had allowed the *prana* in the oxygen levels of the *vayu mandala* to drop below a certain level, large animals and flying insects would not have found the energy to survive and if I had allowed the levels to increase slightly, trees, herbs and all vegetation would have started burning. Everything on this planet, including you, O Shining Fire god, has evolved inside my life systems. Whenever something tries to harm the rest of life, the rest of the system will undo or balance it any way it can."

Having uttered these words, Sita closed her eyes and plunged into the burning ocean. The black waves tossed her body with violent motion; Hanuman and Shabari watched in concern as she became a tiny speck that disappeared into the seething furnace of waters. However, the waters parted in a matter of seconds to reveal a Sita whose dimensions challenged the arc of vision. The sun and moon were her eyes; the firmament her resplendent face, the flowing rivers her tresses, Mount Kailash and Mount Meru her breasts, the spreading deserts of the world her loins, the minerals and ores her limbs of insuperable strength and the surviving species of the plant kingdom her green raiment. A lotus of incomparable beauty grew out of her navel. A radiant smile bloomed on her full lips as she emptied the dark contents of the flaming ocean into her throat.

Agni prostrated before the blue-throated goddess and transformed himself into the digestive fire in her that destroyed the poison she had imbibed from the ocean. Ravana made a clumsy move to salute her. Fumbling awkwardly, he retrieved a byte of memory stored in his hundredth head under the file name, "The Great Oral Traditions of Planet Earth" and intoned:

May those born of thee, O Earth,

Be for our welfare, free from sickness and waste.

Wakeful through a long life, we shall become bearers of tribute to thee.

Sita smiled, acknowledging the ancient lines from the *Prithvi Sukta*.

The ocean lost its fury and anointed her feet with its chrysoberyl waters. The drama was over, and the danger, past. As Sita resumed her human dimensions, the ocean king parted his waters to reveal the bridge of stones painstakingly laid by Rama and his monkey friends.

Sita smiled in anticipation of the small drama which awaited her. The gentle rain which the heavens were sprinkling would revive Rama and bring the ten-headed Ravana back from hiding. Lotus-eyed Rama would later proclaim that he fought the war not to save her but to protect dharma. Struggling to camouflage the anguish in his soul, he would declare before all and sundry, "Sita, let not the world insinuate that Sri Rama's wife is unchaste, having spent ten long months in the palace of Ravana! Let Agni deva pronounce your purity! Only then can you return to Ayodhya as my queen."

And Agni, who would hasten to be a witness in the ordeal dictated by Rama, would again learn a lesson or two about her incendiary potential. Scorched by the fire of her chastity, Agni would be forced to shift shape into a shower of delicate jasmine flowers.

Sita laughed aloud. The epic twist amused her. Fire ordeals, myopic husbands and queer rakshasas were, after all, signposts in this epic journey of disintegration from the one to the many and the returning impulse of reintegration from the many to the one.

Bards recreating the epic in different times and places would express concern about humankind's straying away from the ancient, fundamental relationship to the centre. As antidote to the sense of disconnect in the human psyche, they would compose paeans to the unconditional love that would heal the primal wounding of an unresolved past. The wise among them would recognise the Ramayana heroine as the all-pervading centre and also as their own body. The less enlightened would search for her in the periphery fields heavily marked by duality, hyper-separated as good and evil. All representations and misrepresentations about her would, nevertheless, lead to the implanting of a source seed in human consciousness and for the first time, the children of Prajapati would understand the interrelationship of parts and interdependence of systems.

This was her hypothesis. Sita wondered if it would be included in the alternative *Ramayana* traditions under the title Sita's hypothesis in a new chapter called *Prithivi Khanda*- the earth song. The *Phala Shruti*, the accrued merit for the listener, would be many years of abundant dwelling in the hallowed *Rama rajya* where the rains fell on time and everyone lived in peace and harmony.

Sita's laughter echoed in the hills and valleys of Ravana's kingdom. Hearing it, Ashoka, the sorrowless tree, rejoiced and the crimson *rama bana* flowers emerged from their long underworld sleep.

Hector, O, Hector!

(My tribute to the blind bard Homer, of yore)

A.V. Koshy

Dr A.V. Koshy, Assistant Professor, English, Mount Carmel College, Bangalore, is a poet, critic, and fiction writer. He has 26 books to his credit, **The Art of Poetry (2013), Scream and Other Urbane Legends (2017), Wine-Kissed Poems (2020), and A "Sonetto" for the Poetic World (2022),** *to name a few.*

Hector dressed up that morning, for war
Wore his helmet, ready to kill.
The gates of Troy wide ope, on a hill
Like the gates of heaven, for the poor, at will.
His wife came to him, trembling
Her eyes swimming
And laid her head on his bosom
Aware that, soon, he may Death's groom, become.
Humans are blessed with no knowledge of the morrow.
Hector embraced her and assuaged her sorrow.
Outside, a ten thousand warships had come

At the folly of a younger brother who wanted some fun.
Hector asked her to bring him their son
Who was just a babe, and she did run
To the nursery, and brought him anon.
He started to cry, seeing the warrior grim.
Hector, and she, laughed at his fear
What children fear adults don't want to hear.
Hector took off his helmet, drear.
The child smiled, as he saw his father.
That moment of domestic felicity
Made Hector pray for a better Troy
Where his son would leave a golden reign behind
Than he ever had. But fate was unkind.
Hector was killed by Achilles, and dragged
Around his own city. His men watched, terrified.
His son became no king, his wife died in misery.
Ages later, I praise Hector; for his bravery.
This scene of a soldier, and his wife
His son, and a war, and a prayer with no answer
Asks when humans will give up strife
For peace, so there's no need for a storyteller.

The Editor's Workshop

> Merely pointing out the similarities and differences between characters and events in an earlier version and a mythical rendering would be rather myopic in terms of analysis and interpretation. Properly perusing a text would mean an in-depth study of the myth involved in combination with any relevant literary theory or recurrent concepts (cultural studies, feminism, postcolonialism, hegemony, gender studies, for instance) that offer scope for logical and plausible interpretation.

Voicing the Voiceless: Views on *The Penelopiad*

Lakshmi Krishna Kumar

> **From the Editors**
>
> We now present a reader's views on Margaret Atwood's novel, *The Penelopiad*. However, views alone cannot constitute a research paper. So, here are guiding hints from our end to help you collate observations, citations, and interpretations to produce a collage of mythopoeic perceptions. Thanks to Lakshmi Krishna Kumar for 'voicing' her opinions and for agreeing to be as informal as possible. *Quotations for Analysis and Interpretation, Points to Ponder, Questions to Ponder,* and *References* are from us to help you develop your ideas and delve in-depth into the text.

Questions to Ponder

Every article on myth concerning a literary work starts with a brief introduction to myth and mythmaking. Following this, general information is presented about the text, its treatment of myth, and its rationale. So, how does Krishnakumar present her introduction?

Myths share a cultural and religious significance, which is at the heart of every telling and retelling. Myths have often been accused of being androcentric – of binding women to certain stereotypes. For instance, chastity is one of the most significant terms employed to harness women across centuries. According to Margaret Atwood, Homer's Odyssey is no different from any other myth that deals with gender hegemony. Atwood's attempt to brood over the inconsistencies in the narration of Odysseus has resulted in one of her remarkable works The Penelopiad, the epic of Penelope.

Questions to Ponder

If you were the reader voicing your views on *The Penelopiad* in the form of a research article, what more would you add to the introduction? Choose from the list below and feel free to add your points.

- ✓ A few quotes about myth and mythmaking
- ✓ Representation of society and gender in myths
- ✓ Examples of renowned male-dominated myths

Quotes for Analysis and Interpretation

...in the archaic societies, where, on the contrary, "myth" means a "true story" and, beyond that, a story that is a most precious possession because it is sacred, exemplary, significant... Today... the word is employed both in the sense of "fiction" or "illusion" and in that familiar especially to ethnologists, sociologists, and historians of religions, the sense of "sacred tradition, primordial revelation, exemplary model." (Eliade, 1963, p. 1) – *Myth and Reality* by Mircea Eliade

The word "mythology" comes from the Greek muthos, meaning "story" and logia, "knowledge." Myths tell of the creation of the world or predict its end; they explain how animals were made and the land formed; they bridge the world of humans and the world of the spirits or gods; they try to impose order on a terrifying chaos, and to confront the mysteries of death. Crucially, myths are also the foundation of religions: they define cultures and codify their values. (Introduction, para 2) – *The Mythology Book* – Anonymous

A myth is an account of the deeds of a god or supernatural being, usually expressed in terms of primitive thought. It is an attempt to explain the relations of man to the universe, and it has for those who recount it a predominantly religious value; or it may have arisen to 'explain' the existence of some social organization, a custom, or the peculiarities of an environment. (Spence, 1921, p.3) – *An Introduction to Mythology* by Lewis Spence

Questions to Ponder

- ✓ Which one of these quotes would you use for your introduction?
- ✓ Would you choose a quotation from the list to use in any other part of the paper? If so, where?

The Penelopiad is, in every sense, the epic of Penelope because the story starts and ends with her. There are strong markers in the text that make us view the Homeric narration anew. Atwood questions the credibility of the oral tradition by lending a strong voice to the hitherto muted character of Penelope in Homer's *Odyssey*. The narration presents a sharp contrast between Penelope and the maids on the one hand, and the characters of Odysseus and Telemachus on the other, thereby presenting societal, cultural, and gender differences between the female voice and the male voice.

Questions to Ponder

- ✓ What kind of narration are we looking at, in *The Penelopiad*?
- ✓ Is it a feminist narrative that we see in the novel?
- ✓ What is feminist narratology?
- ✓ What are the seminal texts on feminist narratives that you may require for a research article?

Resources on Feminist Narratology

Lanser, S. S. (1986). Toward a Feminist Narratology. *Style*, 20(3), 341-363. http://www.jstor.org/stable/42945612

Warhol, R. (2005). Feminist narratology. In (Eds.) D. Herman, M. Jahn, & M-L. Ryan. *Routledge encyclopedia of narrative*. Routledge.

Woodiwiss, J., Smith, K., & Lockwood, K. (Eds.) (2017). *Feminist narrative research: Opportunities and challenges*. Palgrave Macmillan.

Quotes for Analysis and Interpretation

From Atwood's Introduction to *The Penelopiad*

"I've chosen to give the telling of the story to Penelope and to the twelve hanged maids... The story as told in *The Odyssey* doesn't hold water: there are too many inconsistencies" (Introduction, para 4)

Penelope's Views on the Homeric version

...I turned a blind eye. I kept my mouth shut; or, if I opened it, I sang his praises. I didn't contradict, I didn't ask awkward questions, I didn't dig deep. I wanted happy endings in those days, and happy endings are best achieved by keeping the right doors locked and going to sleep during the rampages. (A Low Art, para 5)

Penelope Decides to Tell Her Own Story

Now that all the others have run out of air, it's my turn to do a little story-making. I owe it to myself. I've had to work myself up to it: it's a low art, tale-telling. Old women go in for it, strolling beggars, blind singers, maidservants, children – folks with time on their hands. Once, people would have laughed if I'd tried to play the minstrel - there's nothing more preposterous than an aristocrat fumbling around with the arts – but who cares about public opinion now? (A Low Art, para 7)

In the third chapter, the father-daughter relationship enlightens Penelope's mistrust of men. Events like her father throwing her into the sea and the ducks saving her, show how insignificant she is, in the eyes of her father. Atwood hints at the preparedness of the father to murder his daughter because he doesn't want his daughter to be the cause of his death as per the words of the prophecy. Later, Icarius attempts to make amends with Penelope, but she is unsure whether he will shove her or bash her to death with a rock.

Penelope's mother is even worse. She is an ocean nymph who doesn't care much for her daughter. Penelope is almost sure that if it wasn't the father, then the mother would have attempted to drown her. All this proves that Penelope has no parental support and this impacts her personality intensely. She learns to be submissive because she hardly has any option.

> **Quotes for Analysis and Interpretation**

Penelope's Views on Her Parents:

"... the thought would occur to me that he might suddenly decide to shove me over or bash me to death with a rock. Preserving a calm façade under these circumstances was a challenge" (My Childhood, para 7).

My mother, like all Naiads, was beautiful, but chilly at heart. She had waving hair and dimples, and rippling laughter. She was elusive. When I was little, I often tried to throw my arms around her, but she had a habit of sliding away... If my father hadn't had me thrown into the sea she might have dropped me in herself, in a fit of absent-mindedness or irritation. (My Childhood, para 8)

The lament of the maids voices the concerns of the working-class women who are bred in dirt to serve the elite. They have no choice but to clean the dirt present in houses and to get morally dirty, even as children, by sleeping with noblemen and their sons. Nevertheless, over time, they master the secret sneer and ways of seduction to lure men.

> **Quotes for Analysis and Interpretation**

The Twelve Maids Talk About Their Lives:

We were told we were dirty. We were dirty. Dirt was our concern, dirt was our business, dirt was our specialty, dirt was our fault. We were the dirty girls. If our owners or the sons of our owners or a visiting nobleman or the sons of a visiting nobleman wanted to sleep with us, we could not refuse. It did us no good to weep, it did us no good to say we were in pain. All this happened to us when we were children. If we were pretty children our lives were worse. (The Chorus Line, para 1)

Points to Ponder

The act of perceiving the feminine as subservient to the masculine, the double standards of morality, and the role of class in degrading women physically and mentally are part of societal ideology or gender hegemony. Given such a situation, it is necessary to avoid a myopic viewpoint of the novel by restricting it to mythmaking. Subsequently, one must relate such incidents to cultural studies for a more balanced perspective.

Resources on Culture/Cultural Studies

Barker, C. & Jane, E.A. (2016). *Cultural studies: Theory and practice.* (5th ed.). Sage Publications Ltd.

Edgar, A., & Sedwick, P. (Eds.). (2008). *Cultural theory: The key concepts.* (2nd ed.). Routledge.

Oswell, D. (2006). *Culture and society: An introduction to cultural studies.* Sage Publications Ltd.

During, S. (2005). *Cultural studies: A critical introduction.* Routledge.

The comparison between the characters of Penelope and Helen is a recurring theme where Penelope is now able to comment on Helen without being overlooked. Penelope admires the character of Helen, irrespective of the underlying jealousy. She secretly admires Helen but is completely aware that she can never become like her. Helen is symbolic of ideal beauty in the classical period. Her beauty can win hearts and spur men to fight wars over her. Penelope admits that she was not as beautiful as Helen and that is probably the reason that she could never voice herself during her existence. Yet, she considers her wisdom on par with that of Odysseus which makes them a great couple. Nevertheless, she declares that she was not as clever as she thought she was. Throughout the novel, she tries to prove her identity not through beauty but through intelligence.

Quotes for Analysis and Interpretation

Penelope's Views on Helen of Troy

She liked to appear in one of her Trojan outfits...She had a kind of slow twirl she would do; then she'd lower her head and glance up into the face of whoever had conjured her up, and give one of her trademark intimate smiles, and they were hers. Or she'd take on the form in which she displayed herself to her outraged husband, Menelaus, when Troy was burning and he was about to plunge his vengeful sword into her. All she had to do was bare one of her peerless breasts, and he was down on his knees, and drooling and begging to take her back. (Asphodel, para 14)

Helen was never punished, not one bit. Why not, I'd like to know? Other people got strangled by sea serpents and drowned in storms and turned into spiders and shot with arrows for much smaller crimes. Eating the wrong cows. Boasting. That sort of thing. You'd think Helen might have got a good whipping at the very least, after all the harm and suffering she caused to countless other people. But she didn't. (Asphodel, para 16)

Penelope's smartness and intelligence in handling the financial affairs of Ithaca are well-presented in the novel. Her desire to present a richer Ithaca to her husband like a dutiful wife and win his appreciation makes readers feel sorry for her because she is never appreciated for her smartness at any point.

Quotes for Analysis and Interpretation

Penelope's Transition to a Dynamic Queen

My policy was to build up the estates of Odysseus so he'd have even more wealth when he came back than when he'd left – more sheep, more cows, more pigs, more fields of grain, more slaves. I had such a clear picture in my mind – Odysseus returning, and me – with womanly modesty – revealing to him how well I had done at what was usually considered a man's business. On his behalf, of course. Always for him. How his face would shine with pleasure! How pleased he would be with me! 'You're worth a thousand Helens,' he would say. Wouldn't he? And then he'd clasp me tenderly in his arms. (Waiting, para 12)

Points to Ponder

Atwood's Penelope is no chauvinist radical feminist who regards all men as her enemies. She sees how women themselves belittle and degrade their own kind. For instance, Helen, her own cousin, never misses her chance to deride her plainness. Her mother never cares much for her. Her mother-in-law and the old nurse Eurycleia are no better. While the former tries to be an interfering busybody in the beginning but gives up later, Eurycleia is mainly instrumental in pampering and spoiling Odysseus and his son Telemachus. Women like her believe that it is the right of aristocratic men to be barbaric, loud, or unmannerly and that there is always time to change one's habits. Her interference results in Telemachus being as proud and spoilt as his father. Given below are two quotations that illustrate Telemachus' double standards in perceiving women. The first demonstrates that being a typical chauvinist, he is not exempt from the beauty bias. The second shows how he treats his mother and what he thinks of her.

Quotes for Analysis and Interpretation

Telemachus Describes Helen

'As radiant as golden Aphrodite,' he said. 'It was a real thrill to see her. I mean, she's so famous, and part of history and everything. She was absolutely everything she's cracked up to be, and more!' He grinned sheepishly. (News of Helen, para 12)

Telemachus Scolds Penelope for Not Welcoming Odysseus

"Oh mother," Telemachus reproached her,
"cruel mother, you with your hard heart!
Why do you spurn my father so —why don't you
sit beside him, engage him, ask him questions?
What other wife could have a spirit so unbending?
Holding back from her husband, home at last for *her*
after bearing twenty years of brutal struggle
— your heart was always harder than a rock!" (*The Odyssey*, Chapter 23, Lines 111-118)

> **Points to Ponder**

Generally, one of the main characteristics of mythmaking is to parody the exalted and the glorified. This could refer to characters or incidents in the 'original' myth. Read the novel and other revisionist renderings of myths to comprehend how this parodying or belittling of the glorified myth takes place.

> **Quotes for Analysis and Interpretation**

Penelope Nullifies An Existing Mytheme

You've probably heard that my father ran after our departing chariot, begging me to stay with him, and that Odysseus asked me if I was going to Ithaca with him of my own free will or did I prefer to remain with my father? It's said that in answer I pulled down my veil, being too modest to proclaim in words my desire for my husband, and that a statue was later erected of me in tribute to the virtue of Modesty.

There's some truth to this story. But I pulled down my veil to hide the fact that I was laughing. You have to admit there was something humorous about a father who'd once tossed his own child into the sea capering down the road after that very child and calling, 'Stay with me!' (The Scar, paras 26, 27)

> **Points to Ponder**

Atwood's Penelope is no chauvinist radical feminist who regards all men as her enemies. She sees how women themselves belittle and degrade their kind. For instance, Helen, her cousin, never misses a chance to deride Penelope's plainness. Her mother never cares much for her. Her mother-in-law and the old nurse Eurycleia are no better. While the former tries to be an interfering busybody in the beginning but gives up later, Eurycleia is mainly instrumental in pampering and spoiling Odysseus and his son Telemachus. Women like her believe that it is the right of aristocratic men to be barbaric, loud, or unmannerly and that there is always time to change one's habits. Her interference results in Telemachus being as proud and spoilt as his father.

To conclude, Atwood spins an enticing narrative with Penelope voicing her feelings vociferously on the one hand and the maids clamouring for attention as marginals. In the retold version, theodicy does exist with Odysseus being reborn each time as a brave warrior only to die a terrible death or to commit suicide. He fears the haunting of the maids and even Penelope beseeches them to leave him alone. But they are not satisfied because marginalisation is an ideology that hasn't been wiped out of society completely even now.

Points to Ponder

A feminist text does not necessarily have to be spiteful or opposing towards the male characters. Despite Odysseus' flaws, Penelope does appreciate his friendly nature and the way he treats her kindly after marriage.

Quotes for Analysis and Interpretation

Penelope Explains the Reasons for Odysseus' Actions

A more serious charge is that Odysseus didn't reveal himself to me when he first returned. He distrusted me, it is said, and wanted to make sure I wasn't having orgies in the palace. But the real reason was that he was afraid I would cry tears of joy and thus give him away. Similarly, he had me locked in the women's quarters with the rest of the women when he was slaughtering the Suitors, and he relied on Eurycleia's help, not on mine. But he knew me well - my tender heart, my habit of dissolving in tears and falling down on thresholds. He simply didn't want to expose me to dangers and disagreeable sights. Surely that is the obvious explanation for his behaviour. (Slanderous Gossip, para 6)

Questions to Ponder

Like myths, revisionist myths also leave a lot of questions unanswered.

- ✓ Did Eurycleia intentionally get the maids hanged because she felt that their loyalty to Penelope would threaten her position in the royal household?
- ✓ Why do Penelope and Odysseus still like each other?

Resources on The Penelopiad

A research paper must be duly substantiated with citations from other critics whose views may mirror ours, or present an entirely different perspective. Given below are a few citations from articles on *The Penelopiad*. Citing these strengthens one's article in the true sense.

The social and cultural construction of gender in accordance with patriarchal expectations and ideologies endows men with superior and dominant positions where nothing forbids them... Whereas for women there are strict guidelines and laws to guard their virtue and honour... (Irshad and Banerji, 2013, p.38)

It is Penelope's voice speaking from the dead which sparks the connection between ancient myth and contemporary reality, for her story is grounded in the domestic details of her life as daughter, wife, and mother, and then as a queen who has to manage her husband's estates on the island of Ithaca for twenty years single-handed. (Howells, 2006, p.10)

Atwood resorts to collage... and juxtaposes... different styles, and genres to disrupt the grand narrative of Odysseus, and the epic form through which it was delivered. In so doing, the narrative of the maids is allowed to surface and to present itself in defiance of the established and canonized structures. In allowing them to haunt her text, Atwood frees herself of all preconceptions about writing and representation. (Elsalam, 2023, p.31)

The Penelopiad suggests that the contradictions and gaps in the epic are the traces of the patriarchal, male-dominant culture's suppression of female traditions. By exposing patriarchy's exclusions and suppression of female traditions that indicate a different construction of sexuality and subjectivity, the novel destabilizes the foundations of the male subject of patriarchal culture. Atwood's reading of the epic through its gaps resonates with Luce Irigaray's call that mythology needs to be reread so as to disclose how patriarchy establishes its norms by debunking and erasing female traditions. (Yurttas, 2017, p.207)

References:

Atwood, Margaret. (2018). *The Penelopiad*. Canongate Canons.

Eliade, M. (1963). *Myth and reality*. Harper & Row.

Elsalam, D.A. (2023). The maids in Margaret Atwood's The Penelopiad: Transgenerational haunting. In *Transcultural Journal of Humanities and Social Sciences,* Vol. 4(3). pp. 27-41. doi:10.21608/TJHSS.2023.309688

Homer. (1996). *The Odyssey*. Trans. Robert Fagles. Penguin Books.

Howells, C. A. (2006). Five ways of looking at The Penelopiad. In Sydney Open Journals. pp. 5-18.

Irshad, S., & Banerji, N. (2013). Deconstructing gender and myth in Margaret Atwood's The Penelopiad. In *Anglisticum,* Vol. 2(3), pp. 35-41.

Spence, L. (1921). *An introduction to mythology*. Moffat Yard and Company.

The mythology book: Big ideas simply explained. (2018). DK.

Yurttas, Hatice. (2017). Reading The Penelopiad through Irigaray: Rewriting female subjectivity. In *Journal of Letters,* Vol. 34(1). pp 205-217.

Lakshmi Krishna Kumar, Head, Department of English (Second Shift), DDGD Vaishnav College, Chennai (India) specialises in American Literature.

Analysing and Interpreting *Sita's Hypothesis*

Sujatha Aravindakshan Menon

> **Let's Get Started**

There is no dearth of literature on the Ramayana and with the advent of revisionist renderings, Sita is often the subject of interest. The title of Rangarajan's story clearly indicates that the story is a retelling of the *Ramayana*. Obviously, Rangarajan does not intend to narrate the entire epic within the confines of a short story. Therefore, one must be prepared for a narrative that pertains to a particular narrateme/ mytheme in the epic that involves Sita, the wife of the protagonist Rama. Further, while reading about a myth, one must always make sure to read the 'original' or earlier version/s of the myth and other revisionist retellings of the same myth. Since it involves Sita, one must also compare and contrast her role in the older versions and later revisionist retellings for a more precise character delineation. This serves as the background to the basic understanding of the text. This is followed by the part where the researcher reads reference materials related to the theme or genre. The transition to analysis and interpretation proceeds from here.

Some researchers prefer to read all their reference materials before proceeding to the actual reading of a text. On the other hand, many prefer to read the text first to 'get a feel' of the authorial depiction and their own responses. This customisation of one's analytical acumen is more individual and cannot be overgeneralised in any sense. There are no hard and fast rules on 'the method' of reading and interpreting. Therefore the guidelines provided here are only suggestive and not prescriptive.

Hints for Analysis and Interpretation

Rangarajan has deployed two sources – the *Adbhuta Ramayana* and the *Hanuman Charitram* for her story. Often, the sources may not be readily available online or in the free domain. In such cases, the researcher has to procure a copy of the source text. However, there are instances (as in this case) where even the source text is not available in English. In such circumstances, the only option is to surf discussion forums like *Quora* as one does not find the reference to Shatanana (Shatakanta) Ravana elsewhere.

Adbhuta Ramayana

This is a separate rendering of the Ramayana by Valmiki. Surprisingly, while the *Ramayana* deals with the heroic exploits and glory of Ram, this version of the *Ramayana* focuses on Sita. From cantos seventeen to twenty-six, the focus is on the following mythemes:

- Sita spurs Ram to fight the war against Sahastra Ravana, the thousand-headed elder brother of the ten-headed Ravana.
- Ram faces defeat at the hands of Sahastra Ravana.
- Sita metamorphoses into Mahakali kills Sahastra Ravana.

- The *'maatrikaas'* (the terrible goddesses) destroy the army of Sahastra Ravana.
- Ram appeases Sita and requests her to assume her 'usual' form.
- Ram, Sita, and Ram's brothers return to Ayodhya.

Hanuman Charitram

This text was composed by the sage Parashara. It deals with the birth and achievements of Hanuman. According to the seventh chapter of the text, Ram receives a warning from the skies that having killed Ravana, he has to fulfil a greater task. There is one who is mightier than him – his elder brother, the hundred-headed Shatakanta Ravana or Shatanana Ravana. Ram goes to vanquish the demon and put an end to him but is made unconscious. Then Sita and Hanuman transform into Mahakali and Panchamukha (the five-faced one) and defeat Shatakanta Ravana. Mahakali annihilates him while Panchamukha makes sure that his blood does not touch the ground. So, in this text, Hanuman plays an equally significant role alongside Sita. Further, Sita invokes the blessings of Ram and says that if she is really a faithful wife who regards her husband as an embodiment of God, then her arrow should kill Shatanana. Saying this, she shoots an arrow at the hundred-headed demon who finally meets his end.

> **Questions to Ponder**

- ✓ The Ashoka Vana episode and the depiction of Sita and other characters is different from the conventional versions of the Ramayana. List the differences that you find in Rangarajan's story.
- ✓ There are common mythemes from the two sources that Rangarajan fuses together in the story. Identify them for a more precise analysis.
- ✓ Why, according to you, are these sources not as popular as Valmiki's *Ramayana* and Kamban's *Ramayana*?
- ✓ What critical theory does Rangarajan rely on for this revisionist retelling (feminism, structuralism, ecofeminism, Marxism, psychoanalysis)? Read between the lines to find the answer.
- ✓ Why does Rangarajan focus on the Ashoka tree and the Rama Bana flowers?
- ✓ Shabari is deliberately presented in the story. Does her identity as a tribal have anything to do with her affinity or love for nature?
- ✓ How is Shatakanta Ravana presented? Why does he say that he is unlike his ten-headed Ravana who lusts after Sita?
- ✓ What does Rangarajan call the *maatrikaas* here?
- ✓ What does Shatakanta Ravana want? What does he symbolise?
- ✓ "Agni prostrated before the blue-throated goddess and transformed himself into the digestive fire in her that destroyed the poison she had imbibed from the ocean." Rangarajan's subtle use of intertextuality can be seen here.

- What do the words blue-throated and poison suggest to you? Do they remind you of a myth related to another deity?
- Rangarajan presents the death of Shatakanta Ravana differently. What is her authorial intention in doing so?
- "Fire ordeals, myopic husbands and queer *rakshasas* were, after all, signposts in this epic journey of disintegration from the one to the many and the returning impulse of reintegration from the many to the one." How would you explain this? Can the same thing be a source of disintegration and reintegration?
- What does the conclusion indicate?

What More?

The answers to the above questions cannot come only from the researcher/ reader. To obtain answers, one has to read research articles and books on the following areas:

- Myth and Mythmaking
- Retellings of the *Ramayana*
- Retellings of the *Ramayana* with specific reference to Sita (E.g. Chitra Divakaruni's *The Forests of Enchantments*, Amish Tripathi's *Sita: Warrior of Mithila*)
- Ecofeminism and Religion
- Ecofeminism and Myth

Suggested Reading

Divakaruni, C.B. (2019). *The forest of enchantments*. HarperCollins India.

Gokhale, N. (2009). *In search of Sita: Revisiting mythology.* Penguin India.

Iyengar, K.R.S. (1987). *Sitayana: Epic of the earth-born.* Samata Books.

Majmudar, A. (2019). *Sitayana.* Penguin.

Nagpal, S. (2011). *Sita: Daughter of the earth.* Campfire.

Pattanaik, D. (2013). *Sita: An illustrated retelling of the Ramayana.* Penguin Books.

Tripathi, A. (2017). *Sita: Warrior of Mithila.* Westland Limited.

Valmiki. (2010). *Adbhuta Ramayana of Srimad Valmiki.* (Chhawchharia, A.K., Trans.). Chaukhamba Surbharati Prakashan.

Who is Shatanand Ravan? Does any such character exist in Ramayana? *Quora.* https://www.quora.com/Who-is-Shatanand-Ravan-Does-any-such-character-exist-in-Ramayana

Deciphering 'Hector, O, Hector!'

A. Yuvaraj

Let's Get Started

Hector is the crown prince of Troy and a dominant character in Homer's renowned epic, *The Iliad*. In fact, the epic eulogises his valour and dignity throughout. Furthermore, Homer concludes *The Iliad* with Hector's funeral. The epithets associated with Hector clearly indicate his greatness as a hero and human being – "shining Hector," "noble Hector," "godlike Hector," "great Hector," and "heroic Hector." Koshy's poem is an intertextual reference to Book Six of the epic where Hector meets his wife and son. Although Koshy's poem claims to praise Hector's valour, do you think that is his sole intention? One must read the original or source text in order to gain further insights on Hector, and make sense of the context in which the epic and Koshy's poem is set.

Who is the Hero?

Homer intended Achilles to be the protagonist of *The Iliad* because he is the most valiant among the Greeks. However, in the Homerian epic, Achilles' name appears 459 times whereas Hector's name appears 517 times. What does this indicate? Is Hector a greater hero than Achilles? Of course, that remains an endless debate. *Quora* has a long list of discussion threads where the majority favour Hector over Achilles. But what makes

Hector a better hero? Well, that is for the reader/ critic to decipher.

Parallel Archetypes

Hector is the archetype of a dutiful and moralistic brother who defends his country and his younger brother despite the latter's follies. In Hindu mythology, we come across the following characters:

- Kumbhakarna (the younger brother of Ravana in the *Ramayana*)
- Karna (the king of Anga, Kunti's son, and Duryodhana's bosom friend in the *Mahabharata*)

How would you interpret them as parallel archetypes of Hector?

Questions to Ponder

? Why does Koshy say, "The gates of Troy wide ope, on a hill/
Like the gates of heaven, for the poor, at will"?
? On the one hand, Andromache is aware that Hector will meet his end. But the next line says that humans have no idea what the future holds in store. Aren't Koshy's contradictory, or is he drawing a line between premonition and precognition?
? Does *The Iliad* make a reference to Hector and his family? Which book of the epic discusses the conversation between Hector and his wife? How different is it from Koshy's poem?

- ? Why is Hector referred to as "Death's groom?" Does Koshy wish to personify death as a female? What other interpretations can you think of?
- ? Does the helmet play a symbolic role in the poem?
- ? Why is the helmet drear? Koshy uses a transferred epithet by employing the adjective drear. What is actually drear (in the poem and in the epic)?
- ? Neither *The Iliad* nor Koshy's poem mentions the name of Hector's wife. Does this imply anything about the status of women in the classical period?
- ? Hector's wife is depicted as dying in misery. Do other texts also present her as dying a sad and lonely death?
- ? What happens to Hector's son Astyanax or Scamandrius? What are the texts in which he is mentioned?
- ? Do you really think the world will not need a storyteller in future if there is peace and contentment, or is Koshy suggesting that the world will not require a storyteller to narrate events of war and bloodshed?

What More?

As a researcher, you may be interested in writing a research article that covers either of these topics:

- ✓ Drawing a Parallel Between Hector and Other Mythical Archetypes
- ✓ Societal Conditions in a Post-war Context
- ✓ The Portrayal of Hector in Revisionist Mythmaking
- ✓ The Ideology of War in the Classical Period

Suggested Reading

Castleden, R. (2006). *The attack on Troy*. Pen & Sword Military Classics.

Farron, S. (1978). The character of Hector in *THE ILIAD*. *Acta Classica*, Vol. 21, pp. 39-57. http://www.jstor.org/stable/24591547

Graziosi, B. (2019). *Homer: A very short introduction*. Oxford University Press.

Homer. (2011). [7 BCE]. *The Iliad*. Harper Press.

Wiss, W.H. (2019, April 19). "Ther nys a bettre knight": Hector as a Medieval Knightly Ideal. *Discentes*. https://web.sas.upenn.edu/discentes/2019/04/19/ther-nys-a-bettre-knight-hector-as-a-medieval-knightly-ideal/

The Critic/ Researcher

Making Sense of Myth and Mythopoeia

Sujatha Aravindakshan Menon

Myth, once relegated to a mere figment of one's imagination, and often labelled a bunch of tall tales of gods and heroes, is presently the dominant genre in the literary tradition. These days, comics, graphic novels, short stories, novellas, and novels are replete with myths of all kinds. However, understanding the roots or origins of myth is a matter of nonchalance even for those who claim to be passionately fond of myths. Reading myths is a fascination for most readers because as Eliade says, "…one "escapes" from historical and personal time and is submerged in a time that is fabulous and trans-historical" (*Myth and Reality*, 1963, p. 192). Reading about myths from historical, theoretical, and thematic perspectives is not half as fascinating for most of us because it is yet another theory. Nevertheless, if one has to understand and appreciate the value of a myth, it is mandatory to read the works of mythographers and theorists on myth.

Any book on myth must necessarily define myth. My own working definition of myth is that it is a compendium of narratives dealing with the actions of supernatural beings and heroic figures endowed with supernatural powers or aided by supernatural forces. I am wary of using the term 'stories' because they apparently push myths into the realm of falsehood and imagination. The word narrative could refer to either a true story or a false one. Therefore, interpreting myths as authentic accounts or tall tales is the reader's prerogative. But a single definition would certainly be constraining considering the volume and depth of the subject at hand. So, here are the definitions and the functions of myths according to theorists and mythographers. Eliade's (1963) definition places myth on a sacred pedestal.

> Myth narrates a sacred history; it relates an event that took place in primordial Time, the fabled time of the "beginnings."... The actors in myths are Supernatural Beings. They are known primarily by what they did in the transcendent times of the "beginnings." (pp. 5-6)

Jung (1968) relates myth to psychology – the realm of the unconscious. "Myths are original revelations of the preconscious psyche, involuntary statements about unconscious psychic happenings, and anything but allegories of physical processes" (p.154). Campbell (1991) refers to a similar concept of myth by accentuating it as metaphorical and symbolic.

> All the gods, all the heavens, all the worlds, are within us. They are magnified dreams, and dreams are manifestations in image form of the energies of the body in conflict with each other. That is what myth is. Myth is a manifestation in symbolic images, in metaphorical images, of the energies of the organs of the body in conflict with each other. (*The Power of Myth*, p. 46)

Segal (2004) in *Myth: A Very Short Introduction* provides a more 'practical' definition: "I propose defining myth as a story. That myth, whatever else it is, is a story may seem self-evident…

Yet myth can also be taken more broadly as a belief or credo…" (p. 4). Kazlev (2021) presents a highly jargonistic definition of myth. "Myth is the anthropocentric and anthropomorphic representation of the Imaginal reality and its psychoid archetypes in terms of material-physical, historical, and Egoic-personal narrative" (p. 31).

I shall end the string of definitions with a relatively simpler definition of Ellwood (2022):

> A myth is a story of gods, heroes, or other exceptional beings, usually set in primordial times or in an alternative world, which establishes in narrative form the basic worldview and values of a society. It sets forth the origin, meaning, and practice of the society's organization, rituals, and codes of behavior. (p. 1)

Having provided a whole list of definitions, let us draw inferences on the nature or characteristics of myth:

- ✓ It is a collection of stories or narratives dealing with gods, heroes and other beings (monsters, demi-gods, magical plants, animals, etc.)
- ✓ It is aetiological in nature. In other words, it offers explanations for the origin or nature of things in the world.
- ✓ The setting of myths may be our world or another world (Heaven, or the Underworld, or Chaos).
- ✓ The time mentioned in myths is primordial time.
- ✓ The supernatural beings portrayed in myths are anthropomorphic (bearing human qualities).

- ✓ Myths are anthropocentric. They focalise on human beings as the highest forms of earthly creation.
- ✓ Myths are didactic for they provide a framework of rules and rituals that are an integral part of social mores.
- ✓ At the surface level, myths are stories about divine beings and heroic figures. But at a deeper level, they are metaphors of themes and concepts that exist in our unconscious mind.

This is not all. Eliade's view that myth is sacred history is a point to be noted. Are all myths entitled to this privilege? Definitely not. Once a religion becomes obsolete or fades into oblivion or becomes a minority religion of a handful of people, then it takes on the second meaning of myth – a piece of fiction, anything that is false. So, classical mythology (with the exception of a minority of Hellenists) in the eyes of most academicians, readers, critics, and literary artists is nothing more than a bunch of fantasy tales. The same can be said of Norse mythology, which is a minority religion. According to the *National Museum of Denmark* website, "Today there are between 500 and 1000 people in Denmark who believe in the old Nordic religion and worship its ancient gods" (para 1).

On the other hand, the narratives of living religions (By living religions, I refer to those that enjoy a dominant status in society.) are reflections of divine history that are not to be questioned (at least, not by its own worshippers). Therefore, in order to elaborate on this, we ought to understand *myth as narrative, myth as ritual, myth as symbol,* and *myth as spirituality.*

Myth as Narrative

Myths seen as representations of *fantasia* are the most popular forms that we see today. With the advent of graphics and multimedia, cinemas and web shows have given human imagination a new tang with their portrayal of settings, gods, mortals, and monsters. Such depictions place myth at the lowest rank – that of entertainment.

Myth as Ritual

Most of our rites and rituals are based on a mythical background. In most Hindu weddings, the Kashi Yatra (the pilgrimage to the holy city of Kashi) is an important ritual. Here, the groom takes an umbrella, wears his sandals, and makes a show of going to Kashi. Following this, the girl's father coaxes him to stay by offering his daughter's hand in marriage. But when questioned about the significance of such rituals, not many have the answer. Most people say, "Our ancestors started it all. We are just following their ways."

When a rite or ritual is performed as part of cultural transmission from one generation to another, the actions are mainly imbibed whereas the rationale behind those actions is not assimilated into the framework of the community's rite and ritual. As a result, only a few possess the knowledge of why a particular rite or ritual is important as a cultural or religious practice. Myths as ritual belong to the realm of ideology, where they wield a 'soft power' of their own. This brings us to the next function of myth as symbol.

Myth as Symbol

The word symbol, simply stated, refers to anything that means more than what it seems. As Jung (1968) rightly points out, "What we call a symbol is a term, a name, or even a picture that may be familiar in daily life, yet that possesses specific connotations in addition to its conventional and obvious meaning" (p. 20). But here, we are looking at life as a moving picture where every action may also be interpreted as a symbol. Let us return to the Kashi Yatra ritual in a Hindu wedding. The groom performs the act of leaving for Kashi with his umbrella and sandals, taking no other worldly possessions with him. This act is symbolic of celibacy or *Brahmacharya*. In performing this act, the groom highlights the fact that he wishes to remain a *Brahmachari* (bachelor) in the pursuit of knowledge.

The gesture of the bride's father stopping the groom and offering his daughter in marriage is symbolic of the next stage of transition – *grihastha* (family life). The bride's father persuades the groom to enter this stage as it entails perpetuation of the familial line. Here is another example. In *Myth and Reality* (1963), Eliade describes the rituals of the Yurok tribes (a group of Native Americans) during the New Year. According to him, the tribes observe certain rituals for twelve days to welcome the New Year. During these days, the priest visits those places where the Immortals performed certain acts and reiterates the actions. In doing so, the priest symbolically dons the role of the Immortals and repeats the actions for the well-being and prosperity of the tribes (p. 44).

Eliade (1961) places symbolism on the same pedestal as myth:

> Symbolic thinking is not the exclusive privilege of the child, of the poet or of the unbalanced mind: it is consubstantial with human existence, it comes before language and discursive reason. The symbol reveals certain aspects of reality – the deepest aspects – which defy any other means of knowledge. Images, symbols, and myths are not irresponsible creations of the psyche; they respond to a need and fulfil a function that of bringing to light the most hidden modalities of being. (*Images and Symbols*, p. 12)

When one perceives myth as a set of symbols, it is ethereal and way above the mundane – as narrative and ritual. But the ignorant mind does not delve into myths to recognise their symbolic value. Therefore, myth as symbol is part of serious study and contemplation. Otherwise, it remains a mere narrative. For instance, Sigmund Freud's extensive study of myths helped him unravel desires related to basic instincts in the human mind.

Cassirer (1944) aptly describes the symbolic position of myth in facilitating human experience and progress. "Language, myth, art, and religion are parts of this universe. They are the varied threads which weave the symbolic net, the tangled web of human experience. All human progress in thought and experience refines and strengthens this net" (p. 25). Remember a symbol that may connote something divine and spiritual to one may represent something entirely different to another from a different culture or religion. In short, symbolism is as customised in every individual as one's laptop is.

Myth as Spirituality

We now reach the category where myth belongs to the realm of the soul. Let me begin by defining spirituality. The *Cambridge Advanced Learner's Dictionary* defines spirituality as "the quality that involves deep feelings and beliefs of a religious nature, rather than the physical parts of life." This definition makes one wonder if myth as ritual can also be seen as a sub-category of the spiritual realm. I know it is difficult to draw a strong line between the two. Nevertheless, myth is a ritual when it is performed as a routine without understanding its significance and symbolic/ metaphoric value. But when its symbolic value is unravelled, then the transcendence takes place. The individual no longer sees narratives but symbols and metaphors.

Myth as spirituality begins to shape itself in the human psyche when the revelation occurs that these symbols are meant to cleanse one's inner being and make one aware of the 'mysteries' of life. It is an initiation of the soul to the journey 'upward.' Campbell's monomyth now holds a different value. The journey is no longer an external narrative fraught with fantasy where valour gains an upper hand (along with other virtues, of course). It is a spiritual journey where we rediscover our primordial past, the significance of the divine plot and the relevance of the characters. Here, valour is one of the spirits fortified by faith, consistency, patience, and determination. Therefore, Heaven and Earth exist within us and we are guided by the cosmic divine at every step once we perceive myth as spirituality. Campbell aptly opines: "No judging deity is required to assign one to this place or that. All is determined automatically by the spiritual weight (so to say) of the reincarnating monad" (Campbell, *Myths to Live By*, p.71). By monad, Campbell refers to the cosmic divine inherent in every one of us.

Let me elaborate further by using the concept of eschatology. Every religion has eschatological myths – myths that describe the end of the world. Ragnarök, in Norse mythology, is the term for the end of the world. During Ragnarök, even the gods are not spared. They destroy, and are in turn destroyed by, the monsters that are destined to bring about their end. For instance, even Odin, the chief of the gods, does not stand a chance against Loki's offspring, the giant wolf Fenrir. When everything is destroyed, the world is set ablaze by the giant Surtr after which the earth sinks into the sea. The apocalyptic depiction of Ragnarök ushers a sense of fear in the reader, especially when the renowned gods meet their end at the hands of monsters. But the silver lining is that Ragnarök is followed by the rise of a new and overwhelming order of gods and mortals.

What does this indicate to a person who interprets myths as doorways to spirituality? The cycle of death and rebirth is evident here. It also indicates how an excess of evil may wreak havoc on the good we have. Ragnarök is not solely a forthcoming external occurrence. It can rage within an individual as well. When one's destructive or evil side begins to dominate, it has serious repercussions on the good as well. At one point, the good within is quelled by the dominant malevolence.

Similar to the cyclical nature of the world's destruction through fire and water, an individual who exhibits destructive tendencies akin to fire would ultimately succumb to his/ her own malevolence and descend into a state of disorder, mirroring the earth's submergence into the depths of the sea. But all is not lost. When an individual engages in rational thinking and makes virtuous choices, it leads to the establishment of an improved world order within, resulting in spiritual growth and advancement.

Christianity also deals with the fight between the binary opposites, good and evil, culminating in the victory of the former over the latter. Then Christ ascends as the divine judge and pronounces each one's fate based on his/ her deeds. The good ascend to Heaven while the evil plummet to the bottomless abyss to be devoured by infernal fire. This, symbolically, marks the beginning of a new world order. A spiritualist will view this as a warning that one must not traverse the path of evil. On the other hand, for the one who treads the path of virtue, heaven is a sure destination.

Zoroastrianism has a different eschatological myth – a myth where the end denotes eternal happiness and transcendence. In the end, the forces of good (as represented by Ahura Mazda) and evil (represented by Ahriman) cross swords and Ahura Mazda wins, while Ahriman and his legion are completely destroyed. After destroying Hell, Ormuzd (another name for Ahura Mazda) purifies Earth using divine fire. As a result, all human beings are bestowed with divinity and immortality. So, one is not promised just a stay in Heaven but also the status of divinity if he/ she chooses good over evil.

Myths therefore demonstrate how death is a portal to a new world and a new way of life. Myths serve as gateways to the unknown mysteries of life. As Karen Armstrong (2005) remarks, "Myth is about the unknown; it is about that for which initially we have no words. Myth, therefore, looks into the heart of a great silence" (What is a Myth? para 4). According to mythographers, silence is another term for primordial time. It encompasses all that is divine, sacred, and permanent.

Having elaborated on the nature and function of myths, it is now necessary to deliberate the concept of mythmaking, otherwise called mythopoeia, mythopoesis, and revisionist writing.

Mythopoeia: Origin and Types

The term *mythopoeia*, which means mythmaking, owes its origin to J.R.R. Tolkien who used it as the title for one of his poems, published in 1931. The entire poem is addressed to his friend C.S. Lewis, who is named Misomythus (one who harbours a disdain for myths). Tolkien, in contrast, proudly calls himself Philomythus (one who loves myths). The poem vividly illustrates the power of imagination in fashioning fantastic worlds, an entirely new pantheon of dazzling gods, enchanting magical creatures, and gruesome, macabre monsters. "Blessed are the legend-makers with their rhyme / of things not found within recorded time" (Mythopoeia: 91-92). In other words, mythopoeia primarily refers to the creation of myths.

Keeping Tolkien's implicit definition of mythmaking or mythopoeia in mind, I would like to categorise mythopoeia into two – generative mythopoeia and adaptive mythopoeia. Generative mythopoeia is where the writer designs a cosmos that is similar to the one found in existing myths but which is the product of a higher degree of ingenuity. Tolkien's *Lord of the Rings* (1954-55) and *Silmarillion* (1977) are the best examples of this type. There is no dearth of writers who have explored and experimented with this genre. J.K. Rowling, David Eddings, Terry Pratchett, Philip Pullman, Roshani Chokshi, Eoin Colfer, George R.R. Martin – the list goes on.

Generative mythopoeia is like constructing a building from the very scratch. Consequently, it involves a greater creative and literary onus on the writer to make sure that everything is in its right place and there are no odd pieces sticking out. Adaptive mythopoeia, on the contrary, is like renovating or modifying an existing construction.

In order to understand adaptive mythopoeia in the right sense, one needs to revisit Coleridge's "Kubla Khan" (1816). In the poem, Coleridge describes the river Alph that flows through caverns and chasms underground and then sprouts as a fountain.

> *Amid whose swift half-intermitted burst*
> *Huge fragments vaulted like rebounding hail,*
> *Or chaffy grain beneath the thresher's flail:*
> *And mid these dancing rocks at once and ever*
> *It flung up momently the sacred river.* (Kubla Khan: 20-24)

If one were to interpret these lines in relation to myth and mythopoeia, then the river Alph represents the 'original' or the older version of the myth. The caverns represent the unconscious mind that abounds with fecund imagination and varied archetypes. Due to the force of imagination, the older myth undergoes modification and re-surfaces as a mythopoeic version.

Just as the fountain flings up rocks along with the sacred river, the mythopoeic version decentres all those mythical characters and events around which the 'original' myths are based. Although it does bear a resemblance to the older version in some ways, the mythopoeic version undoubtedly assumes an identity of its own. This is the second type of mythopoeia – the adaptive.

Since the Classical Age, there have been varied versions of renowned myths and legends. But the last decade of the twentieth century has witnessed a steady rise in mythic retellings, particularly by feminist writers. Although men writers have also been actively involved in revisionist mythmaking either pertaining to women characters or to male characters, the bulk of adaptive mythopoeia largely rests with women writers.

A meticulous scrutiny of a mythopoeic text would require more than the confines of a research paper. But to put it simply, the basic structure of an adaptive mythopoeic text is as follows: the mythemes of the original myth are modified or viewed differently from the writer's point of view or from a marginalised character in the text. The term marginal is mainly used for a character who is at the periphery owing to gender or class. In Sara Maitland's "Andromeda," (1996) and Madeline Miller's "Galatea," (2013) the narrators are none other than the characters themselves. In Margaret Atwood's *The Penelopiad* (2005), the twelve hanged maids play the role of the chorus alongside Penelope, the protagonist and chief narrator. In Kavita Kane's *Lanka's Princess* (2017), the writer dons the role of the heterodiegetic omniscient narrator.

The intent behind a revisionist retelling could be for any of the following reasons:

- ✓ To present a different standpoint that has hitherto been unexplored. This is often seen in those myths where the narrator or character becomes the devil's advocate, either advocating the cause of another mythical character or justifying his or her viewpoint. Anand Neelakantan's *Asura: Tale of the Vanquished* (2012) is the retelling of the famous Indian epic Ramayana from Ravana's point of view. In *Ahalya's Awakening* (2019), Kane defends Ahalya's actions and justifies her 'transgression' by attributing it to other social and psychological factors.

- ✓ To decentre the hero or main character and to replace him/her with a minor female character. This type of adaptive mythopoeia is one of the most predominant modes of literary expression because of its ability to present the marginal as the focal point of the narrative. Circe is a sorceress whose appearance is recorded only in a chapter of Homer's *Odyssey*. But she is the protagonist in Madeline Miller's novel *Circe* (2018), through whose eyes we view the

Greek world, its heroes and how women have to brave hazards to opt for free will in an androcentric society. "Mirrors" (2003) by Shashi Deshpande deals with the myth of Nahusha (a virtuous king who was blinded by arrogance and lust and who was cursed to become a serpent), narrated from Indra's wife Sachidevi's point of view. In the story, the reference is made to yet another marginal – Nahusha's wife, Ashoka Sundari. Sachidevi's reference to Ashoka Sundari is true of most women characters and other marginals in myths and folktales. "You have no place in any of the stories that are being told about what happened, none at all in the court poet's poem. And it is as if you never existed" (Mirrors 76).

✓ To examine social issues such as gender, class, caste, family, power politics, and environmental pollution that have remained in the background or have not been discussed in the 'original' myth. Traditional myths often envelop us in an aura of heroic glory that everything else remains misty and extraneous. The focus on the hero's valour and strength, demonstrated by his ability to vanquish terrible monsters or demons, forms the centre of attention and the entire myth rests on the mythemes pertaining to, or culminating in heroic achievement. But the revisionist retellings focus more on issues pertaining to political or social hegemony as is seen in the novels of Natalie Haynes, Amish Tripathi, Madeline Miller, Chitra Divakaruni, Anand Neelakantan, Sara Maitland, Devdutt Pattanaik, Anuja Chandramouli, Kaitlin Bevis, and Rick Riordan, to name a few.

There is yet another category of adaptive mythopoeia where the main plot remains untouched while the writer exercises liberty to add a few dialogues or descriptions in order to catch the readers' attention. This is the weakest form of mythopoeia where not much is changed. Children's fiction, comics, and storybooks for young adults deal with this type.

To sum up the concept of mythopoesis in the words of Kazlev (2021), "While the archetypes of the Imaginal World are timeless ... the external, historical, material-physical world and socio-cultural structures are constantly changing, and knowledge is always advancing" (Myth – A New Definition, para 7). This creates a disjointedness or disjunction between the Imaginal (the universe of imagination) and the Logical.

> Because of this disjunction, myths, and hence our representation of the sacred, have to be constantly reinvented and re-envisaged in each historical period, and new myths built from older ones, or even created from scratch. This is the task of the mythopoeticist, the myth-maker. (Myth – A New Definition, para 9)

This is true not only of printed texts but also of visual media.

Mythopoesis and the Visual Media

While the film world occasionally excites its audience with a blockbuster fantasy film, the OTT teems with fantasy dramas, each dealing with a mythical world that is designed and set in motion by the screenwriter and the director. Most fantasy dramas are adaptations of printed texts, the most popular example being *Game of Thrones* (2011-2019), which is based on

George R.R. Martin's series *A Song of Ice and Fire* (1996-?). Another example is *The Shannara Chronicles* (2016-2017), based on Terry Brooks' *The Sword of Shannara Trilogy* (1977-1984), which deals with a world consisting of druids, demons, and elves, supported by the sacred tree, the Ellcrys. A few other examples include *The Bride of Habaek* (2017), *Hotel del Luna* (2019), *Fate: The Winx Saga* (2021-2022), *The Bureau of Magical Things* (2018, 2021), and *The Witcher* (2019-2023).

What is interesting to note about generative mythopoeia is that while some texts (printed or visual) deal with an entirely different mythical world characterised by a unique set of rules, divinities and living beings – mortal and magical (*Game of Thrones, The Shannara Chronicles*), others deal with the mythically enchanted world that exists in parallel to the world of humans (*Hotel del Luna, The Bureau of Magical Things*).

Mythopoeia or mythopoesis in the visual media largely caters to the young adult, or the adult, but some films and drama series cater to children too. A close study reveals that more than dramas, animation films cater to 'kids' although they are equally popular among adults. Some of the recent examples of mythopoeic animation films are *Moana* (2016), *Ainbo: The Spirit of the Amazon* (2021), *Raya and the Last Dragon* (2021), and *The Sea Beast* (2022).

As a myth freak, I only have this to say – myths are labyrinthine pathways to the inner depths of our being. The rationalist may pooh-pooh their very existence but it is unimaginable to live a purely rational life like the one in Dickens' *Hard Times*. India's renowned mythographer Devdutt

Pattanaik (2003) is indeed right when he says: "Myths may not satisfy the demands of rationality or science, but they contain profound wisdom—provided one believes they do and is willing to find out what they communicate. That is precisely the purpose of mythography" (p. 160).

To conclude, I would suggest a moderate and neutral approach to myths in order to decode their true nature and implications in our rapidly changing world. Enjoy them as stories, follow them as rituals, decode them as symbols, and internalise their symbolic/ metaphoric value to be in harmony with your own spiritual self. Do all of these or any of these. After all, freedom of will is the best blessing we have received.

References:

Armstrong, K. (2005). *A short history of myth*. Canongate.

Benioff, D. & Weiss, D.B. (Creators). (2011-2019). *Game of thrones*. [Drama; HBO]. HBO Entertainment.

Byung-soo, K. (Director). (2017). *The bride of Habaek*. [Drama; Netflix]. Number Three Pictures.

Cambridge University Press. (2013). Spirituality. In *Cambridge advanced learner's dictionary* (4th ed.). Cambridge University Press.

Campbell, J. (1972). *Myths to live by*. Bantam Books.

Cassirer, E. (1944). *An essay on man: An introduction to the philosophy of human culture*. Yale University Press.

Chung-hwan, O. (2019). *Hotel del Luna*. [Drama; Netflix]. GTist.

Coleridge (1816). Kubla Khan. https://www.poetryfoundation.org/poems/43991/kubla-khan

Deshpande, S. (2003). Mirrors. In *Stories. Vol. 1.* (pp. 76-86). Penguin Books.

Eliade, M. (1961). *Images and symbols.* Trans. P. Mairet. Havrill Publishers.

Eliade, M. (1963). *Myth and reality.* Harper and Row, Publishers.

Ellwood, R. (2022). Myth: Key concepts in religion. Bloomsbury.

Gough, A., & Millar, M. (Executive Directors). (2016-2017). *The Shannara chronicles.* [Drama; Netflix]. Sonar Entertainment.

Hall, D. & Estrada, C.L. (Directors). (2021). *Raya and the last dragon.* [Film; Amazon Prime Video.]. Walt Disney Pictures, Walt Disney Animation Studios.

Hissrich, L.S. (Creator). (2019). *The witcher.* [Drama; Netflix]. Little Schmidt Productions, Hivemind.

Jung, C.G. (1964). Approaching the unconscious. C.G. Jung (Ed.), In *Man and his symbols* (pp. 18-103). Anchor Press.

Jung, C.G. (1968). *Archetypes and the collective unconscious.* Trans. R.F.C. Hull. (2nd ed.). Princeton University Press.

Kazlev, M. A. (2021) *Mythopoesis and the modern world.* Manticore Press. Kindle Edition.

Musker, J. & Clements, R. (2016). *Moana.* [Film; Amazon Prime Video]. Walt Disney Pictures, Walt Disney Animation Studios.

Pattanaik, Devdutt. (2003). *Indian mythology: Tales, symbols, and rituals from the heart of the subcontinent.* Inner Traditions International.

Segal, R.A. (2004). *Myth: A very short introduction.* Oxford University Press.

Shiff, J. M. (Creator). (2018). *The bureau of magical things.* [Drama; Netflix]. Jonathan M. Shiff Productions.

The old Nordic religion (asatro) today. *National Museum of Denmark.* https://en.natmus.dk/historical-knowledge/denmark/prehistoric-period-until-1050-ad/the-viking-age/religion-magic-death-and-rituals/the-old-nordic-religion-today/

Tolkien, J.R.R. (1931). Mythopoeia. http://vrici.lojban.org/~cowan/mythopoeia.html

Young, B. (Executive Producer). (2021). *Fate: The Winx saga.* [Drama; Netflix]. Archery Pictures.

Williams, Chris. (Director). (2022). *The Sea Beast.* [Film; Netflix]. Netflix Animation.

Zelada, J. & Claus, R. (Directors). (2021). *Ainbo: The spirit of the Amazon.* [Film; Amazon Prime Video]. Tunche Films, Katuni Animation.

Ahalya's 'Awakening' in the Twenty- First Century

Anjitha Anil and Sushant Kishore

Indian epics like the *Ramayana* and the *Mahabharata* hold immense cultural, social, religious, and national significance. A comprehensive understanding of Indian society's history and contemporary culture necessitates knowledge of these grand Indian epics. In support of their greatness, Tagore affirms that it is insufficient to merely acknowledge the *Ramayana* and the *Mahabharata* as two exceptional epics; they also serve as a historical account, albeit not tied to a specific era. Instead, they embody the eternal history of India (Sakalani, 2004, p. 51). The importance of these classical texts transcends time, remaining relevant to-date and continuing to inspire generations.

Indian society has undeniably been entrenched in patriarchy since ancient times, a fact that becomes glaringly apparent when examining classical texts. The *Ramayana* and the *Mahabharata* predominantly centre around Lord Vishnu's avatars Rama and Krishna. Even important female characters such as Sita and Draupadi are silenced and moulded to support the development of the main male characters. They serve as passive agents who trigger transformational life events in these characters. This approach by Valmiki and Vyasa has faced continuous scrutiny from modern readers. As perspectives evolve, even established binaries of good and evil begin to shift. Consequently, numerous writers have embarked on a quest of retelling these epics, akin to a yagna, unveiling hidden and neglected perspectives.

Women have occupied a marginalized position in religion, myth, and history, but social movements like feminism have empowered them to move from the periphery to the centre. Literature serves as a mirror reflecting society, and previous works penned by men perpetuated patriarchal ideologies. Therefore, advocates of movements like feminism have harnessed literature as a medium to propagate progressive ideas. Women's writing has gained significant prominence by resurrecting silenced female characters from the grand Indian epics and giving voice to their concerns. The victims of male-dominated narratives now rise like phoenixes from their ashes, reclaiming their true identity and challenging patriarchal norms.

Kavita Kane, an acclaimed female novelist, offers a fresh perspective on the grand Indian epics through a feminist lens. Her notable works include *Karna's Wife* (2014), *Sita's Sister* (2014), *Lanka's Princess* (2017), *Menaka's Choice* (2015), *The Fisher Queen's Dynasty* (2017), *Ahalya's Awakening* (2019), *Saraswati's Gift* (2021), and *Tara's Truce* (2023).

Kane's writing aims to redefine traditional gender standards by challenging the negative effects of patriarchy. *Ahalya's Awakening* (2019), in particular, presents the tale of Ahalya in the *Ramayana* from a feminist perspective. In recent years, several writers have examined the epic through the eyes of characters such as Sita, Ravana, Surpanakha, Mandodari, Urmila, Kaikeyi, and others. However, Kane takes a unique approach by focusing specifically on Ahalya, a minor character overshadowed by the central figures of the narrative. In the *Ramayana*, Ahalya's sole purpose is to serve as a tool to glorify Rama and showcase his greatness. She is portrayed as a sinful woman who is later redeemed by Rama's mercy. Her significance in the epic is limited to a single episode, and she has no further role beyond reflecting Rama's kindness and divinity through her redemption.

Ahalya's Awakening (2019), in other words, seeks to rewrite the male-centric version of Ahalya's story as narrated by Valmiki. This paper aims to analyse the character of Ahalya through comparison and contrast of Valmiki's *Ramayana* and Kane's *Ahalya's Awakening* (2019). In other words, through this paper, the authors intend to provide insights into how the dominant patriarchal system has suppressed and distorted the narratives of female characters, perpetuating a male-centric worldview.

> 'Even a fool can marry,' she added contemptuously. 'A woman is like a slave.' 'That *is* extreme!' remarked Gautam, regarding her closely. 'Yes, like a slave. We are nothing but the legal property of our fathers or husbands or brothers, and are forced to obey them. And when a woman has to marry against her wishes, it is slavery. She is not free to choose. She has to submit.' (Chap. 7, The Ashram)

There are different versions of the story of Ahalya in the Puranas and the *Ramayana*. In the *Bala Kandam* or the first part of *Valmiki Ramayana*, Ahalya, the wife of the sage Gautama, is visited by Indra in her husband's guise. Despite seeing through his guise, she succumbs to his desires. As retribution for their sins, Gautama curses Indra to be deprived of his scrotum (testicles), while Ahalya is cursed to stay invisible for a thousand years only to be redeemed by Rama's presence in the hermitage. When Rama enters the hermitage and touches Ahalya's feet, she is redeemed from her curse. In turn, she touches his feet as a sign of reverence and is lauded by the celestials from above since she would be under Gautama's control once again. Gautama returns to be happily reunited with Ahalya (pp. 116-118).

According to the *Uttara Kanda* of *Valmiki Ramayana*, Ahalya is innocent and does not see through Indra's disguise. She also questions Gautama on why she has to be punished when she knew nothing about Indra's tricks. Brahma himself tells Indra in the *Uttara Kanda* that he fashioned Ahalya himself. So, she is *ayonija sambhava* (born without the womb).

> I made a female, who on account of the grace of her limbs became known as Ahalya ; " Hala " meaning ugly, from which " Halya " is derived, and she in whom " Halya" does not appear is named Ahalya; this was the name I called her. (p. 476)

The *Bhagavata Purana*, Skanda IX, book 21, verse 34 describes Ahalya as the daughter of Mudgala, the king of the Puru clan, and the twin of Divodasa (p. 1236). Kane's novel, *Ahalya's Awakening* (2019) is based on the *Bhagavata Purana* and the *Bala Kanda Ramayana*.

Kavita Kane's novel, "*Ahalya's Awakening*," presents a distinctive style by shifting the focus from Rama to Ahalya. The story unfolds from the perspective of Menaka, an apsara from Indralok. Menaka recounts the tale to Nahusha, the new Indra, in an attempt to dissuade him from forcing himself on women, emphasising the impending misery.

The narrative begins with Ahalya's birth as one of King Mudgal and Queen Nalayani's twins. Ahalya stands out as the most beautiful child on earth, overshadowing her twin brother, Divodas. Despite Guru Vashisht recognising Ahalya's intelligence, her parents prioritise her beauty over her intellect.

Indra Shakra befriends Divodas and uses this connection to frequently visit and stay in the palace, secretly desiring Ahalya. However, his chauvinistic attitude and narrow mindset often displease her. Although a marriage proposal is presented to her parents, Ahalya's true passion lies in seeking knowledge and becoming a *rishika*. Eventually, she convinces her parents to allow her to pursue her ambitions under Rishi Gautam's tutelage in his ashram.

During her stay at the ashram, Ahalya and Gautam develop romantic feelings for each other, but before they can express their love, she is called back to her palace due to the ongoing war. Her mother intends to get her married to Indra, but Lord Brahma intervenes, suggesting a *swayamvar*. Gautam wins the contest, but he agrees to marry Ahalya only if she willingly accepts him as her husband. Although Nalayani is heartbroken, Ahalya accepts the proposal, and Indra, despite causing a commotion, acknowledges the sage's victory.

After marriage, Ahalya finds herself burdened by domestic chores and raising their four children, leaving little time for academic or romantic pursuits. She becomes disheartened, feeling undesirable and unappreciated, especially when compared to Indra's devoted wife, Sachi. In the words of Mondal (2021), "In fact, this desire to contain and eliminate the feminine is present in Ahalya's marriage itself, that quarantines her sexual urges in an "uncultivable" marriage and later into an inanimate stone" (p. 25). Eventually, Indra approaches her as a friend, sensing trouble in her marital life. Initially, Ahalya rejects his advances, but surrenders to his disguised presence since she yearns for the passion and love that is lacking in her marriage. However, Gautam catches them together and curses Indra, leading to his eventual redemption in the Himalayas.

Gautam also curses Ahalya, making her invisible to humans, surviving on air and ashes until she finds redemption. But before cursing her, there is an argument between the two of them where Ahalya questions his neglect of her feelings.

> I am not an infallible being, I am not a god, I am a woman!' she said furiously. 'Is it that when a woman is not "good," she does not receive sympathy? Do I have to be perfect to deserve that sympathy? I was not.'

> 'Nor was I,' he reminded her, his face rigid. 'No one has to be perfect to be deserving of justice. I have no right to judge you. I couldn't make you happy, I couldn't keep you happy,' he said. 'If it was your desire, perhaps even your vanity, then it was my arrogance, my negligence, that failed both of us.' 'You realise all this now?' she said

painfully, her voice low. 'Not when I pined and pleaded for your attention? Did I have to do this to gain it, losing myself, my respect, my everything?' Her lips curled in a bitter sneer. (*Ahalya's Awakening*, Chap. 24, The Parting)

Kane presents this incident as part of her mythopoeic rendering. In the other versions like the *Brahma Vaivarta Purana*, the *Adhyatma Ramayana*, and the *Skanda Purana*, Ahalya patiently bears the curse and Rama is ultimately portrayed as the saviour. Kane's novel mentions Ahalya's salvation in Rama's presence, yet there is no happy reunion. Although Gautam seeks to reunite with her, Ahalya decides to live independently, refusing his proposal. Towards the end of the novel, Ahalya meets Sita in the forest, and they both reflect on society's cruel treatment of women while granting men various privileges.

In Valmiki's epic, Ahalya is either portrayed as a stone, or a stone-like passive object whose significance revolves around three men: Indra, who instigated her to defy societal norms; Gautam, who punished her for infidelity; and Rama, who liberated and restored her life. Kane's Ahalya challenges this male-centric narrative and allows Ahalya's silenced voice to be heard, enabling her to share her life story.

Kane, on the other hand, portrays Ahalya as not just the beautiful creation of Lord Brahma; but also an articulate, complex, intelligent, courageous, and self-assured woman with a clear purpose in life – to become a *rishika*. Unlike most women of her time, she rejects the idea of finding happiness through a marriage of convenience. Instead, she chooses to marry an ascetic like Gautam, the man she truly loves and who, she thinks, can help her become a *rishika*.

Initially, Ahalya's married life seems like a dream come true, but it quickly turns into disillusionment. Gautam becomes engrossed in his work, leaving her feeling moody, melancholic, and sexually unfulfilled. In other words, she is a source of disappointment to her parents, as she neither becomes a *rishika* nor fulfils their ideal of marrying a suitable man.

When Indra reappears in her lonely life, she believes he genuinely loves her and desires him. When he disguises himself as Gautama, she finds the fulfilment she craves for, resulting in her transgression. However, when Gautam discovers their affair, Indra abandons her without concern, leaving her to realise that his true feelings were merely lustful. As Ottilingam et al (2021) opine, "Sexual fidelity should not be considered only …. a female prerogative. The male's fidelity in … marriage is as important as that of the female." (p.370)

Fidelity does not merely refer to the loyalty in the physical sense, but a sense of trust and moral support towards one's spouse. Gautam, who previously justified the adultery of another rishi's wife, finds it difficult to accept Ahalya's actions and punishes her without considering his broken promises. The world denounces her, and even more painful to Ahalya is her family's indifference as they abandon her.

During her period of punishment, Ahalya finds her true self and experiences profound peace. "She [Kane] also endows Ahalya with temerity to commit a transgression, and then accept its consequences. She empowers her with the ability to comprehend human desire, coupled with spiritual awakening" (Sahasrabuddhe, 2019). Kavita Kane empowers Ahalya to accept her transgression and its consequences, allowing her to comprehend human desire alongside spiritual awakening.

Kane adopts the redemption of *Valmiki Ramayana* where Ahalya liberates herself and chooses to return to her original form in the presence of an enlightened soul like Rama. Kane paints Ahalya as strong-willed and self-reliant, a quality not inherent in the previous versions of the *Ramayana*. The meeting between Ahalya and Sita at the end of the novel provides closure to the story of two women victimised by patriarchy, abandoned by their husbands. However, this reciprocity is not arrived at spontaneously.

The epilogue is an unwinding of not only women's relationships with the men in their lives and society at large but also women's relationships with other women. Both these women, Ahalya and Sita, have been victims of "other's transgressions" and the "pride...[and an] inflated sense of honor as a man, as a husband, as a rishi or as a king", but this experience has not endowed them with empathy for one another, and other women (Kane, 2019, p. 254). It is after a series of barbed questions, sardonic remarks and scornful glances that the similarity of their experiences dawns on them. This forest, cut off from the realms of men - courts, cities, kingdoms and civilisation, is a "more truthful place" that allows a space for reflection, introspection and dialog removed from the moral diktats of men (Kane, 2019, p. 258).

Kane exposes the hypocrisy of both Rama and Gautam, who justified the infidelity of other men's wives but failed to accept their own wives' actions when questions arose regarding their chastity. Marriage, as society's normative way to control women, becomes a tool to limit the power of strong women like Ahalya. Kane's novel advocates for women like Ahalya to break free from societal constraints and carve out their own identities.

Unlike Valmiki, Kavita Kane presents Rama and Gautam as multidimensional characters, with shades of both white and black. Instead of blindly criticising them and Indra, she accuses the male-dominated society as the main cause of their follies. In addition to Ahalya, Kane sheds light on the sufferings of Sachi and Sita, two women who endure the tribulations of a patriarchal society.

Through her storytelling, Kane effectively transforms Ahalya into a dynamic character with whom one can relate to, even at present. Ahalya symbolises the modern woman who is in complete charge of her body, mind, and life. In the words of Desai (2023),

> Ahalya, a prominent figure in Hindu mythology, begins her narrative within the confines of patriarchal norms. She is the wife of sage Gautama and finds herself ensnared in a tale of transgression and transformation. Her myth centres on a pivotal moment when she is seduced by Lord Indra, the king of the gods, who disguises himself as her husband. This act of deceit leads to her husband's curse, turning her into a stone statue- a punishment for her perceived infidelity… However, her

awakening becomes emblematic of her defiance against these societal constraints. (p.194)

References

Bose, M. (2004). *The Ramayana revisited*. Oxford University Press.

Kane, Kavitha. (2019). *Ahalya's awakening*. Westland Publications. Epub.

Mondal, I. (2021). Sexing the Devi: Morphology of the mythic fantastic in Ahalya(s) and Chitrangada(s). *International Journal of English and Studies*. Vol. 3(12), pp. 20-28.

Ottilingam, S., Suresh, T.R., & Raghavan, V. (2021). The legend of Ahalya: A midnight imposter at the hermitage. *Journal of Psychosexual Health*, Vol. 3(4), pp. 367–370.

Sahasrabudhe, A. (2019, August 30). In Ahalya's awakening, Kavita Kane questions the penalty for infidelity, and its significance in Indian mythology. *Firstpost*. https://www.firstpost.com/living/in-ahalyas-awakening-kavita-kane-questions-the-penalty-for-infidelity-and-its-significance-in-india

Sakalani, D. (2004). Questioning the questioning of Rāmāyaṇas. *Annals of the Bhandarkar Oriental Research Institute*, 85, 51–65. https://www.jstor.org/stable/4169194

Shastri, J.L. (Trans. and Ed.). (1999). *The Bhagavata Purana*. Motilal Banarsidass Publishers.

Valmiki. (1892). *The Ramayana: Balakandam*. (M.N. Dutt, Trans.). Deva Press.

Valmiki (1952.). *The Ramayana of Valmiki*. (Shastri, H.P., Trans.). Vol. 1-3. Shanti Sadan.

Sushant Kishore, Assistant Professor, VIT, Vellore, specialises in South Asian Studies. Anjitha Anil is a research scholar at VIT, Vellore. Her area of research is Indian mythological fiction.

Exploring Mythmaking in Chokshi's
Star-Touched Stories

A.R. Chitra

Chokshi as a Mythic Literary Artist

Indian mythology has a deep meaning for Roshani Chokshi, who frequently uses it as the inspiration for her works. Chokshi being of Indian descent, incorporates elements of Indian mythology, folklore, and cultural traditions into her storytelling. In response to a question, she says:

> I was really inspired by the childhood stories that my grandmother told me. To me, they were so rich with details and texture that it really shocked me how these worlds and mythologies were never explored in mainstream literature. I was particularly inspired by Greek and Hindu mythology. (Sophie, 2018)

These mythological themes provide a rich backdrop for her stories and add layers of connotation to her narratives. Her debut novel, *The Star-Touched Queen*, reimagines the Hades and Persephone tale in an Indian environment. Chokshi gives her retellings distinctive twists and interpretations thereby imbibing new life into classic tales.

Chokshi often features powerful female characters in her stories, drawing inspiration from the strong and fierce goddesses of Indian mythology. These characters embody the strength, wisdom, and divine actions of Indian goddesses like

Kali, Durga, and Lakshmi. By incorporating myths into her writings, Chokshi not only breathes new life into ancient tales but also makes them relevant to contemporary readers, fostering a deeper understanding and appreciation of Indian mythology.

As a Western writer, Chokshi approaches Indian myths through her cultural lens, offering interpretations and adaptations that reflect her understanding and creative vision. Although her narratives may not offer an all-encompassing picture of Indian mythology, she attempts a dissemination of its cultural significance in a global context.

Myth and Culture

Myth and culture are deeply interconnected, with myths serving as an integral part of a culture's beliefs, values, and identity. They provide explanations for the origin of the world, the creation of humans, and the existence of natural phenomena. Myths often feature deities, supernatural beings, and heroic figures that are central to any society's religious, spiritual, and moral practices. They are a means of transmitting cultural knowledge from one generation to the next and carry narratives of historical events, ancestral wisdom, and societal norms.

Through storytelling, rituals, and oral traditions, myths ensure the preservation of cultural heritage, values, and customs. Malinowski (1948) rightly states, "Myth fulfils in primitive culture an indispensable function: it expresses, enhances, and codifies belief; it safeguards and enforces morality; it vouches for the efficiency of ritual and contains practical rules for the guidance of man" (p.79).

Myths contribute to the formation of a collective identity within a culture. They provide a sense of shared history, cultural pride, and a common narrative. In addition, they embody cultural norms, ethical codes, and social hierarchies. "The society that cherishes and keeps its myths alive will be nourished from the sound set, richest strata of the human spirit" (Campbell, 1973, p.13). Mythological characters/ stories serve as archetypes, exemplifying virtues / vices, and providing moral guidance for individuals within the spectrum of culture.

Rituals often re-enact mythological events or honour mythological figures, reinforcing cultural traditions and religious practices. They provide a symbolic framework for understanding myths by imbuing them with meaning and significance. Myths address fundamental questions about the nature of existence, the human condition, morality, love, power, and the pursuit of meaning. They serve as a bridge between the past and present, and act as a testament to the richness and diversity of human civilisations.

Star-Touched Stories

Star-Touched Stories is a captivating collection of novellas that draws readers into the enchanting and mythical world of fantasy. In a tapestry of three enthralling novellas, Chokshi explores love, destiny, and the power of the supernatural. These narratives portray the lives of well-known as well as unfamiliar personalities, providing glimpses of their adventurous, transformative, and revelatory journeys.

In *Death and Night*, Chokshi explores the relationship between the two central characters, Dharma Raja, and Night. Chokshi's narrative shifts between Bharata and the rich and magical Night Bazaar. Dharma Raja and Night are complex, multidimensional characters with their fears, desires, and encumbrances. Furthermore, Chokshi's portrayal of the divine and mythical beings alongside the lovers adds an element to the narrative.

Poison and Gold introduces readers to Aasha, a Vishakanya. "For a vishakanya, all it took was one touch to end a mortal life" (*Poison and Gold*, Chap. 1, para 3). Here, Chokshi explores the intricacies of the Vishakanya lore and weaves a myth around Aasha's toxic bloodline.

> As a vishakanya, she might have a deadly touch, but she had another power too. She could read the desires of others. All she had to do was reach forward with part of her mind, and card through a human's intentions as if they were cloth. (*Poison and Gold*, Chap. 1, para 12)

As a Vishakanya, Aasha grapples with her lethal powers and seeks a way to rid herself of her deadly touch. Her struggle with self-acceptance and the desire for freedom is relatable and adds depth to her journey.

Rose and Sword is about Gauri and Vikram who embark on a perilous journey filled with illusions, riddles, and tests of courage. Here, Chokshi creates a vivid and immersive setting, transporting readers to the kingdoms of Bharata and Ujjain, with their rich cultural tapestries and mystical elements. The dynamics between the two main characters, Gauri and Vikram, is the highlight of the story. The story explores how individuals can shape their paths, even in the face of adversity.

Mythological and Archetypal Criticism

Mythological criticism often examines the role of rituals and rites of passage, which mark important transitions or milestones in a person's life. These rituals can be seen as expressions of mythic patterns and serve to reinforce cultural values and beliefs.

Through the analysis of rituals, mythological critics gain insights into a text's underlying themes and the cultural context in which it is embedded. It involves studying similarities and differences between different mythologies and their recurring motifs or archetypes. By comparing myths from various cultures, scholars can identify common themes and understand how human experiences and cultural values are expressed and shared across different societies.

Mythological criticism often draws on psychological theories, particularly those of Carl Jung and Northrop Frye, who believed that myths and symbols are manifestations of the collective unconscious. Jungian analysis explores the psychological dimensions of myths and their relevance to individual and cultural psychology. It examines how mythic narratives reflect universal human experiences, desires, fears, and the quest for self-realisation.

Archetypal criticism focuses on the analysis and interpretation of archetypes within literary works. Archetypes are recurring symbols, motifs, characters, or narrative patterns that are found across different cultures and periods. These archetypes represent fundamental human experiences, emotions, and themes that reverberate with readers on a deep and universal level. "An archetypal symbol is usually a natural object with a human being, and it forms part of the critical view of art as a civilized product, a vision of the goals of human work" (Frye, 1957, p. 112).

Archetypes are fundamental and universal patterns of thought, behaviour, and symbolism that are deeply ingrained in the collective unconscious of humanity. They represent common human experiences, desires, fears, and motivations. Examples of archetypes include the hero, the mentor, the villain, the journey, the quest, and the mother figure. These archetypes can be found in myths, folklore, fairy tales, and literature from various cultures.

The concept of the collective unconscious, as proposed by psychologist Carl Jung, is central to archetypal criticism. The collective unconscious refers to the shared reservoir of inherited experiences and knowledge that all humans possess. Archetypes are believed to emerge from this collective unconscious and influence our understanding and interpretation of the world around us. Archetypal criticism emphasises the symbolic nature of literature. These symbols carry deeper meanings beyond their literal interpretation, representing universal concepts or ideas. For example, a snake might symbolise temptation or transformation, while a journey can represent personal growth or self-discovery.

Roshani Chokshi's *Star-Touched Stories* is characterised by allusions to various myths, particularly Indian. The novellas feature recurring mythic motifs and archetypes that smack of universal human experiences. In the story *Death and Night*, the character of Night embodies the archetype of a powerful, enigmatic deity associated with darkness and mystery. Night's character and her realm evoke the universal archetype of the primordial goddess. An archetype warrants symbolic meanings within a text, exploring how myths and symbols are employed to convey abstract ideas, moral values, or psychological states. Symbols can be objects, actions, or events that carry deeper significance beyond their literal interpretation. For example, a serpent may symbolise temptation or knowledge, while a journey can represent self-discovery or transformation.

Transformation

In mythology, the theme of transformation serves as a metaphorical tool to explore spiritual growth, and emphasise the transformative potential within individuals. Stories from world mythologies contain instances of magical transformations. In Greek mythology, Daphne transforms into a laurel tree to escape Apollo's pursuit, symbolising her desire to remain chaste and free from his advances. In Egyptian mythology, Osiris is murdered by his brother Seth but is later resurrected and transformed into the god of the underworld, representing death and rebirth.

In Native American mythology, Coyotes frequently go through transforming experiences that teach them adaptation, ingenuity, and the dual nature of things. Norse mythology tells the story of Loki who frequently transforms into various creatures, reflecting his trickster nature and his ability to shape-shift.

In Chokshi's collection, characters and places undergo transformation. For instance in *Death and Night*, Dharma has the power to transform darkness/ nothingness into a magical horse:

> I twisted the dark in my hands, and thought of the Tapestry and the Shadow Wife's curse. When I opened my eyes, I faced what my thoughts and energy had created: A lustrous horse with milk-pearl eyes. It drew its lips back over its teeth and in the unshaped dark of its mouth, a city glinted—steel spires and iron trees, paved walkways of jasper and agate, squares of amber windows glittering in the makeshift night. A hidden world. (*Death and Night*, Chap.1, Death)

Many characters undergo physical transformations that represent their inner journeys. For example, Night ventures into the realms of the Otherworld. This transformation symbolises a shift in identity, breaking free from constraints, and embracing their hidden potential. "For as long as I had lived, I had always belonged to two worlds. My duties nourished the human world, and there I learned my dances. My life belonged to the Otherworld, and there I learned my duties. But I was Night. And it meant that I was forever a threshold, a space between past and present, yesterday and tomorrow" (*Death and Night*, Chap. 4, Night).

In *Poison and Gold*, the protagonist Aasha's journey represents a transformative quest for self-discovery and redemption. The mythical transformation of the Vishakanya is a prominent element in the novella. In Hindu mythology, a Vishakanya is a mythical creature, often portrayed as a poisonous maiden or a woman with venomous abilities. Chokshi weaves the concept of the Vishakanya into her fictional world, thereby exploring the theme of transformation. Aasha undergoes a profound transformation, both physically and emotionally. Vishakanyas are often depicted as women who are infused with poison, either through birth or through a ritual. This poison imbues them with lethal abilities, making their touch or presence toxic to others.

Aasha seeks to break free from the constraints of her identity as a toxic creature and seeks love, acceptance, and a sense of purpose. The transformation represents a metaphorical journey of reclaiming humanity, transcending societal expectations, and embracing one's true self. It reflects the power of personal growth, self-acceptance, and the potential for change, even in the face of seemingly insurmountable obstacles.

Vikram in *Rose and Sword* grapples with the transformative power of choice as he questions and reshapes his destiny, ultimately altering the course of his own story. Love and connection serve as catalysts for transformation in many of the stories. Characters find strength, solace, and a sense of purpose through their relationships, allowing them to restructure in terms of their perspectives, priorities and values.

Rites and Rituals

Rites and rituals are frequently examined as manifestations of legendary patterns in mythologies. The novella *Rose and Sword* features a wedding ceremony imbued with symbolism, representing a significant rite for the characters involved. The rituals in this novella connect to cultural and mythological traditions surrounding marriage. Each ritual bears significance, highlighting themes of transformation, destiny, and the supernatural elements of Chokshi's mythopoeic world.

In *Poison and Gold*, Aasha the Vishakanya, goes through a ritual called the *Sangarsh*. It tests her abilities and marks her transition into adulthood. In *Rose and Sword*, the protagonist Vikram undergoes a ritual involving a divine rose and a magical sword. This ritual represents a rebirth and renewal of his purpose and identity, as he embraces his destiny as the prince of a fallen kingdom. According to Watson-Jones and Legare (2016),

> Because rituals are group-specific, socially stipulated actions, they are an effective means of demonstrating phenotypic similarity and thus allow individuals to determine potential cooperators in extended networks. For example, engaging in approved social etiquette and participating in group-specific ceremonies allow the identification of in-group members. Rituals provide signals that individuals share similar beliefs and values and therefore are more likely to be trustworthy reciprocators. (p.43)

Mythic Love

Archetypal criticism explores the theme of mythic love and the concept of soul mates. The story *Death and Night* portrays a mythic love story between Night and Dharma, the god of death. Their connection transcends time and death, representing the archetype of soul mates, who are destined to be inseparable. Characters in Chokshi's novellas experience a sense of recognition and an inexplicable bond with each other across different lifetimes. They are drawn to one another, and their love persists over time, reinforcing the idea of a timeless connection.

Mother Figure

Generally, the mother figure represents nurture, wisdom, and protection. While not all novellas in the collection explicitly feature a mother figure, there are instances where maternal figures are portrayed. In *Rose and Sword*, the protagonist Vikram recalls his mother, the late Queen of Bharata. Her love, strength, and sacrifices shape Vikram's character and influence his decisions as he faces challenges and seeks to restore his fallen kingdom. In *Poison and Gold*, both Aasha and Vikram reflect on their respective mothers' legacies. While the mother figures may not always be physically present, their impact resonates through memories and inherited wisdom, showcasing the significance of maternal bonds and their transformative power in the characters' journeys.

Underworld Journey

World mythology is replete with legendary heroes venturing into the underworld. In *Rose and Sword* Vikram, faces trials and tests in the underworld. These challenges test his character, bravery, and determination as he seeks to restore his fallen kingdom. Vikram's underworld journey symbolises his growth, self-discovery, and the sacrifices he is willing to make for his people.

> Beside her, Vikram's eyes were wide. He walked beneath this sea of paper transformations, blank pages that looked like the beginning of a tale. The painted stars didn't shine, but Vikram regarded them as if they were real and somehow, the light changed. The force of his wonder was its own illumination. (*Rose and Gold*, Chap. 8, Second Blush)

These journeys are transformative, as characters confront their fears, gain wisdom, and emerge changed from their experiences in the Otherworld. In the words of de Resende and Martinez (2020),

> …the concept of katabasis may be associated, symbolically, with the comprehension of the existence of a double nature in man, which would involve two dimensions: on the one hand, a material one, and on the other, a spiritual one. Taking into consideration body aging changes and the possibility of death, it is quite fair to question/inquire/ ponder if the limits and purposes of human existence are genuine when one realizes about the human body aging changes and the possibility of death. In this context, religions seek to provide answers and rituals to deal with these questions about the ultimate reality. The transition from a material to a spiritual realm,

embodied by death, would then represent an experience of katabasis and anabasis, or vice-versa. (p.88)

Conclusion

Roshani Chokshi's *Star-Touched Stories* takes readers on a captivating journey through mystical and enchanting worlds. The exploration of mythical themes, such as transformation, destiny, and love, transports readers to a realm where gods and mortals coexist, and the boundaries between reality and fantasy blur.

References:

Campbell, J. (1973). *Myths to live by.* Bantam Books.

Chokshi, R. (2018). *Star-Touched stories.* St. Martin's Press. Epub.

de Resende, P.H.C. & Martinez, M.D. (2020). C.G. Jung's katabasis: From ancient myths to modern visionary experiences. In *Junguiana*, Vol. 38(1), pp. 87-100.

Frye, N. (1957). *Anatomy of criticism: Four essays.* Princeton University Press.

Malinowski, B. (1948). *Magic, science and religion and other essays.* The Free Press.

Sophie. (2018, August 07). Star touched stories by Roshani Chokshi: Q & A. *Beware of the Reader.* https://www.bewareofthereader.com/star-touched-stories- by-roshani-chokshi-q-a/

Watson-Jones, R.E., & Legare, C.H. (2016). The social functions of group rituals. In *Current Directions in Psychological Science*, Vol. 25(1), pp. 42–46.

A.R. Chitra, Assistant Professor, Sastra Deemed-to-be University, Thanjavur (India), holds expertise in Post-colonial Studies, Cultural Studies, and Feminism.

Book Reports/Reviews

Robert A. Segal's *Myth: A Very Short Introduction*
A Book Report

Fr. Joby Joseph

> **From the Editors**
>
> You must be wondering why a book published almost two decades ago must be mentioned here. The answer is simple. *Myth: A Very Short Introduction*, as the title implies, presents an overview of myth and its application to various disciplines. But do not let the title and the size of the book mislead you, as the information presented, although relatively minuscule, is more than one can ask for. Therefore, it is a must-read for research scholars and those interested in myth, religion, and cultural studies. We hope this detailed synopsis will inspire myth-lovers and researchers to use the book as a launchpad for extensive reading.

Robert Segal is primarily known for his expertise on myth and religious studies. Therefore, it is not surprising that this seemingly 'small' book provides a treasure house of information on myth. Segal begins by clearly stating the aim and purpose of the book. "… this book is an introduction not to myths but to approaches to myth, or theories of myth, and it is limited to modern theories. Theories of myth may be as old as myths themselves" (p.1).

The book is divided into eight chapters, each of them relating myth to a specific discipline. The first chapter 'Myth and Science', deals with the concept of creationism where myth can also be viewed as a science since it deals with creationism as well. In addition, it can also be viewed as primitive science because it explains the cause of physical events (storms, earthquakes). Although these events are attributed to divine powers and have fallen low in the eyes of science and secularism, it is a kind of primitive science as well. Segal here cites the significant role played by E.B. Tylor, James Frazer, Lévy-Bruhl, Malinowski and Claude Lévi-Strauss, Robert Horton and Karl Popper in interpreting myths.

In the second chapter titled 'Myth and Philosophy', Segal in the Keatsian style says that "myth is philosophy... philosophy is myth... myth grows out of philosophy... philosophy grows out of myth" (p. 36). Here, the views of Paul Radin, Ernst Cassirer, the Frankforts, Bultmann and Jonas, and Albert Camus are briefly discussed. On the whole, myth is seen as a branch of knowledge, which further endorses the fact that myth is a philosophical tale.

Segal in the third chapter, 'Myth and Religion,' refers to two main tactics that are employed to reconcile myth and science by attempting to reconcile religion and science. The first strategy is to consider religion as symbolic and to proclaim that most events mentioned in religious texts have been deemed unscientific because they have not been interpreted symbolically. The second strategy is to give secular phenomena religious undertones and thereby place them on the same pedestal as religion. Since the agents involved are not supernatural forces, such religious undertones will have no contradictions with science. In this chapter, Segal deals with the Romanian religious historian Mircea Eliade and his views at length. The names of Bultmann and Jonas recur here since they view myth as symbolic.

'Myth and Ritual' is the fourth chapter of the book. Here, Segal presents a contrast between William Robertson Smith and E.B. Tylor. While Tylor sees ritual as secondary to myth, the former sees myth as secondary to ritual. According to Smith, myth is best understood only through ritual. Frazer's views on ritual are highlighted here, particularly the ritual related to the birth and rebirth of the god of vegetation, and the ritual related to the killing of the king. Harrison and Hooke, Girard, and Burkert are other veterans whose views feature here.

Segal begins his fifth chapter, 'Myth and Literature' thus: "The relationship between myth and literature has taken varying forms. The most obvious form has been the use of myth in works of literature" (p. 79). In this chapter, he cites the views of Jessie Weston, Northrop Frye and Lord Raglan. Weston relates the Grail myth to the myth of vegetation, death and rebirth. Frye claims that all literature stems from the myth of the hero and relates the genres of literature to the seasons. According to Segal, myth is valued in literature for its story value. Lord Raglan, whom most of us may not have known at all, is mentioned here for his morphology of the hero myth that consists of twenty-two narratemes.

'Myth and Psychology' is one of the most interesting chapters because it looks at myth from the viewpoint of three renowned minds – Sigmund Freud, Carl Gustav Jung, and Joseph Campbell. Freud uses the myth of Oedipus to explore the hidden desires of a man who wishes to ravish his mother as Oedipus did. But unlike Oedipus who manages to fulfil his desires, human beings cloak their basic impulses using the ego and the superego.

Freudians like Karl Abraham, Ranks, Jacob Arlo, Bettelheim, and Alan Dundes are discussed in this chapter. While discussing Jung, Segal brings up the concept of heroism. For Jung, heroism involves a relationship with the unconscious. The difference between Jung and Campbell is that while Jung considers heroism as the first part of the hero's life, Campbell considers the second part as heroic.

The mythic hero Adonis, who recurs in almost every chapter, is mentioned here too. In Jung's view, Adonis is the archetype of the eternal child or the *puer aeternus*. The puer is someone who wishes to remain a child under the protection of his mother. Adonis prefers to be under the protection of his mother, and the goddesses who are attracted to his beauty. However, a puer never evolves, and so he dies a premature death like Adonis. "The opposite of the puer archetype is that of the hero. The hero succeeds where the puer fails" (p.111).

The seventh chapter 'Myth and Structure' is mainly centred around the theories of the French anthropologist, structuralist, and mythographer, Claude Lévi-Strauss. Out of the thirteen pages allotted to the chapter, seven pages focus on

Lévi-Strauss' theories of myth. According to Segal, Lévi-Strauss' views on myth are threefold. Firstly, myth is the least orderly of the humanities. At the same time, it is not an outcome of boundless imagination but that of "scientific-like processes of observation and hypothesis" (p. 114). Secondly, like most anthropologists, he also considers myth a primitive phenomenon, but an exquisite one. Lastly, myth does not deal with opposites but provides solutions to resolve conflicts between them. Following Strauss' views are those of Vladimir Propp, Georges Dumézil, and the Gernet School.

'Myth and Society' forms the last chapter of the book that focuses on the views of Malinowski, Sorel, and Girard. According to Malinowski, myths deal with social phenomena like marriage, ritual, family, community, etc. "Social myths say, 'Do this because this has always been done.' In the case of physical phenomena, the beneficiary of myth is the individual. In the case of social phenomena, the beneficiary is society itself" (p. 127). Sorel, on the other hand, sees myth as a tool that seeks to end the present social order. It is similar to the revolution of the socialists – to put an end to the existing capitalist society and to give rise to a new one. In Girard's view, myth is not a means of ending social structure, but one that tries to resolve aggression and violence.

In the conclusion, Segal presents a parallel between play and myth and emphasises that myth is mostly a make-believe. But despite its status as make-believe, such myths serve as guides to a better understanding of the world. Further, not all myths are make-believe. Many of them are sacred truths. The last part of the conclusion deals with the world of cinema where heroes and heroines are deified. The last lines are remarkably appropriate in the present set-up. "Cinema-going combines myth with ritual and brings gods, hence myths, back to the world – and does so without spurning science" (p. 142).

To sum up, Robert Segal's book is anything but a very short introduction. It is a mini encyclopedia in its own right. What is interesting is that Segal repeatedly dwells on the Adonis myth in most of his chapters by analysing it from a psychological, religious, ritualistic, structural, and monomythical perspective. It is a ready reckoner for those who wish to know all about theories and theorists associated with myth. Readers who succeed in reading the book will surely find the intellectual depth of its contents transferred to their eager minds.

Source:

Segal, R.A. (2004). *Myth: A very short introduction*. Oxford University Press.

Fr. Joby Joseph, Assistant Professor, Kuriakose Elias College, Kottayam (India), specialises in Comparative Literature, Postmodern Fiction, and Portuguese Literature.

Anand Neelakantan's *Nala Damayanti*

R. Durga and S. Barathi

Anand Neelakantan is a celebrated writer of revisionist mythmaking. *Asura: Tale of the Vanquished* (2012), *Ajaya: Roll of the Dice* (2013) and its sequel *Ajaya: Rise of Kali* (2015), *Vanara: The Legend of Baali, Sugreeva and Tara* (2018), and *The Bahubali Trilogy* (2017-2020) are some of his well-known works. His recent work, *Nala Damayanti: An Eternal Tale from the Mahabharata* (2023), is based on the timeless tale of Nala and Damayanti.

The novel is highly captivating and a compelling read. Neelakandan's characters are so lively and fascinating that they effortlessly find their way into the minds of the readers. The novel is loaded with *opsis* that one can mentally visualise the entire story scape. The book *revolves* around Nala, the king of the Nishadhas, and Damayanti, the princess of Vidharba, and the way destiny unites them despite all obstacles.

Nala is described as an efficient king interested mainly in the welfare of his subjects and redefining their identity by making them more civilised. Damayanti is not the usual princess or damsel in distress but a brave, beautiful, and free-willed woman. Although the novel is titled *Nala Damayanti*, it is Hemanga and Rituparna who steal the show. Hemanga, the golden swan from Brahma Lok, is not merely a messenger but almost a second protagonist in the novel. Rituparna is not just a fat old king who spends his time drinking and merrymaking but a guru who teaches Nala life's lessons amidst laughter and amusement. He often reminds one of Shakespeare's fools or clowns who prove wiser than most of the main characters. "Live as if you are going to die the next moment and live as if you are going to live forever… you need no God, heaven, or hell other than what you make in your mind" (Chapter 23, The Three Gods Again).

Nala Damayanti addresses diverse social issues like gender discrimination, superstitions, subalternity, and hegemony. In fact, Neelakantan attributes the inferiority complex in Nala to his subaltern status. His characterisation is so powerful that he makes the readers empathise with the characters in the face of adversity. The novel portrays most of the characters with a tinge of modernity, making them question societal issues that are more relevant to the contemporary set up.

In short, *Nala Damayanti* is a real page-turner for those of us who love to have our nose in a book.

Source:

Neelakantan, A. (2023). *Nala Damayanti: An eternal tale from the Mahabharata*. Kindle ed., Penguin Random House India Private Limited.

S. Barathi, Assistant Professor, Sastra Deemed-to-be University, holds expertise in Diaspora Studies, Children's Literature, and Ecocriticism. S. Durga, a research scholar at Sastra Deemed-to-be University is pursuing her research in the mythopoeic novels of Kavita Kane.

Natalie Haynes' *Stone Blind*

A. Yuvaraj

Natalie Haynes is essentially known as a writer of revisionist mythmaking, the proof of that being her popular novels, *The Children of Jocasta* (2017) and *A Thousand Ships* (2019). *Stone Blind: Medusa's Tale* (2022) is Haynes' latest novel, which is also longlisted for the Women's Prize for Fiction 2023. Usually, reviews are overall objective analyses of a text. This review intends to be no different. At the same time, it adopts a more structured approach by examining the novel from the viewpoint of the elements of fiction.

Plot

Stone Blind is a novel where the main plot dealing with Medusa's life intersperses with the sub-plot concerning Athena and Perseus to create a narrative confluence. At the periphery are the other Olympian deities each preoccupied with his or her interests. The exposition/ birth of the three characters is catchy and remarkable.

Character

The novel has a whole medley of characters – the gorgons, the gods, a talking crow, the Nereids, Perseus, Cepheus and his family, the olives, and even the snakes. Since the novel is centred around Medusa, Haynes portrays only the Gorgons as round characters. The others hardly change their spots although there is a hint of change in Athena at the end of the novel before her metamorphosis. Anthropomorphism, which is generally a defining feature of deities in mythology, is intensified to such an extent in *Stone Blind* that one begins to view the Greek pantheon with revulsion. The description of the Gorgons and their love for Medusa is touching and incites empathy in the reader.

Generally, mythopoeic narratives depict heroes who are glorified in patriarchal narratives as ordinary, egoistic men. In this novel, Perseus, who is glorified as a hero in older myths, is reduced to laughing stock. For the most part, he is deemed useless and ignorant by Hermes and Athena who are sent to help him.

Setting

The setting is diverse and adds enchantment to the novel. It shifts between Mount Olympus, the caves by the sea where the Gorgon sisters live, the dwelling place of the Hesperides, the island of Seriphos, the temples of Athena and Poseidon, and the palace of Cepheus.

Theme

Identifying the theme of a novel is an open-ended question that invites a medley of answers from readers and critics. Generally speaking, Haynes intends to highlight the role of divine hegemony in twisting the fates of mortals. She also presents the helplessness of female characters – goddesses and mortals – who are forced to succumb to the will of the patriarchal gods. In her opinion, the solution to this raging issue is Medusa's metamorphosed state.

Narrator

Haynes shares her narratorial role with Panopeia, who is one of the Nereids. Panopeia, as her name implies, is omniscient and sees everything that happens to the characters. But this is not all. The polyphony of narratives is taken up by another unnamed Nereid, Cornix a talking crow, *Elaia* the olives, and Herpeta, the snakes that adorn Medusa's head.

To sum up, Natalie Haynes' *Stone Blind* is a reincarnation of the older myth where the concept of a monster is redefined and the perceiver is forced to revise his/ her mindset to welcome Medusa as she is, into the post humanist world.

Source:

Haynes, N. (2022). *Stone blind*. Picador.
https://read.amazon.com/?asin=B09VGZJ8RY&ref_=kwl_kr_iv_rec_2

Afterword

Now that we have reached the end of the book, it is necessary to provide a befitting afterword, which in turn, is the 'teaser' to yet another venture. Despite the growing interest in myth, the key function of myth in the present set-up is as entertainment mainly due to its relation to fantasy and magic. The visual media has made sure of this, the proof of it being the OTTs that teem with fantasy dramas, not to discount the role of printed texts.

The increasing popularity of the mythopoeic genre can be attributed to the following reasons:

- ✓ They don't disturb religious sentiments because they are distanced from reality. This is evident in Tolkien's poem 'Mythopoeia' (1931) where he justifies his act of creating gods, heroes, and an entirely new world. "I bow not yet before the Iron Crown,/ nor cast my own small golden sceptre down" (Mythopoeia: 129-130). This is a clear indication that Tolkien neither intends to abdicate his faith nor his creativity.
- ✓ Mythic creations or renderings mentally transport us to a different world where we imagine ourselves to be a character in the book/ drama.
- ✓ They fill us with a sense of euphoria and often teach us soft skills like conflict resolution, negotiation, people management, and the like. The converse is equally true that it does instigate some of us to indulge in violence, trickery,

and falsehood. But this is true not just of fantasy literature (print or visual) but all forms of literature. Here again, it is the human mind and not the medium that is at fault.

- ✓ For those of us who look beyond, some of the characters become quintessential heroes, heroines, friends, lovers, and teachers whom we end up imitating, emulating, or even defending. This also includes those who teach us how not to be. They are symbols that inspire, guide and warn us in our daily lives.
- ✓ They question our belief in stereotypes and through their dynamic character delineation, teach us to be more open-minded in viewing the world and its inhabitants. For instance, submissiveness is perceived as a feminine quality but not a defining quality at that. Again, courage is not the defining characteristic of a man nor is it restricted to the masculine gender.

A gentle suggestion to those of you who wish to delve deep into the theories of myth – Never carry the burden of the 'original myth.' All myths are modified before they reach another set of audiences. This has been the case right from the Classical period. Therefore, any mythopoeic rendering has every right to dignity and significance as much as its predecessor. As Armstrong (2008) aptly remarks,

> When Freud and Jung began to chart the modern quest for the soul, they instinctively turned to classical mythology to explain their insights, and gave the old myths a new interpretation. There was nothing new in this. There is never a single, orthodox version of a myth. As our circumstances change, we need to tell our stories

differently in order to bring out their timeless truth. (*A Short History of Myth*, para 12)

I desire to base my next book to generative mythopoeia with specific reference to the visual media. Since researchers have started working on dramas and films for their master's or doctoral research, there is a pressing need for reference books related to myth and the visual media. I hope the Muses guide me in my ventures so that I may emerge successful with yet another book that duly serves its purpose.

Sujatha Aravindakshan Menon

www.ingramcontent.com/pod-product-compliance
Lightning Source LLC
LaVergne TN
LVHW061616070526
838199LV00078B/7307